The Garland Library
of Medieval Literature

General Editors
James J. Wilhelm, Rutgers University
Lowry Nelson, Jr., Yale University

Literary Advisors
Ingeborg Glier, Yale University
Guy Mermier, University of Michigan
Fred C. Robinson, Yale University
Aldo Scaglione, University of North Carolina

Art Advisor
Elizabeth Parker McLachlan, Rutgers University

Music Advisor
Hendrik van der Werf, Eastman School of Music

Seven Medieval
Latin Comedies

translated by
ALISON GODDARD ELLIOTT

Volume 20
Series B
GARLAND LIBRARY OF MEDIEVAL LITERATURE

Garland Publishing, Inc.
New York & London
1984

Library of Congress Cataloging in Publication Data
Main entry under title:

Seven medieval Latin comedies.

(Garland library of medieval literature ; v. 20,
ser. B)
    Bibliography: p.
    1. Latin drama, Medieval and modern—Translations
into English.   2. Latin drama (Comedy)—Translations into
English.   3. English drama (Comedy)—Translations from
Latin.   I. Elliott, Alison Goddard.   II. Title: 7 medieval
Latin comedies.   III. Series: Garland library of medieval
literature ; v. 20.
PA8165.S48   1984   872'.03'08   83-49077
ISBN 0-8240-9414-X (alk. paper)

Printed on acid-free, 250-year-life paper
Manufactured in the United States of America

For Rick and Mark
who have given me such joy

The Garland Library
of Medieval Literature

Preface of the General Editors

The Garland Library of Medieval Literature was established to make available to the general reader modern translations of texts in editions that conform to the highest academic standards. All of the translations are original, and were created especially for this series. The translations attempt to render the foreign works in a natural idiom that remains faithful to the originals.

The Library is divided into two sections: Series A, texts and translations; and Series B, translations alone. Those volumes containing texts have been prepared after consultation of the major previous editions and manuscripts. The aim in the editing has been to offer a reliable text with a minimum of editorial intervention. Significant variants accompany the original, and important problems are discussed in the Textual Notes. Volumes without texts contain translations based on the most scholarly texts available, which have been updated in terms of recent scholarship.

Most volumes contain Introductions with the following features: (1) a biography of the author or a discussion of the problem of authorship, with any pertinent historical or legendary information; (2) an objective discussion of the literary style of the original, emphasizing any individual features; (3) a consideration of sources for the work and its influence; and (4) a statement of the editorial policy for each edition and translation. There is also a Select Bibliography, which emphasizes recent criticism on the works. Critical writings are often accompanied by brief descriptions of their importance. Selective glossaries, indices, and footnotes are included where appropriate.

The Library covers a broad range of linguistic areas, including all of the major European languages. All of the important literary forms and genres are considered, sometimes in anthologies or selections.

The General Editors hope that these volumes will bring the general reader a closer awareness of a richly diversified area that has for too long been closed to everyone except those with precise academic training, an area that is well worth study and reflection.

James J. Wilhelm
Rutgers University

Lowry Nelson, Jr.
Yale University

Contents

xi

GENERAL INTRODUCTION

The seven texts translated here were probably all written in the twelfth century. It is, however, possible that *The Three Girls* dates to the early thirteenth century, and the very late eleventh century is barely possible for *Pamphilus* (see Dronke, 1979).* The authors whose names are known — Vitalis of Blois, William of Blois, Arnulf of Orléans, and Matthew of Vendôme (whose *Milo* is not included) — all come from the Loire valley in France. French origin is also likely for the others, although Peter Dronke's suggestion concerning the importance of Tegernsee for *Pamphilus* deserves careful consideration, and the author of *Babio* may have been English.

The Latin comedies constitute an important, but rather neglected, group of texts. They reveal the fascinating complexity of twelfth-century culture. While their debt to the thought and poetry of classical antiquity is great — so great indeed that some of them have been ascribed to Ovid — they could only have emerged in what C. H. Haskins called the twelfth-century Renaissance. The comedies show the extent to which classical culture had been memorized, assimilated, and then transformed into something new, something wholly medieval. *Geta* and the *Aulularia*, for instance, employ a classical plot as a vehicle for satirizing the medieval philosophical schools. Combining philosophy and obscenity in *Alda*, William of Blois injected ideas gleaned from Bernard Silvester into a scabrous tale which Boccaccio found worthy of imitation (Goldin). Others utilized substantial borrowings from classical

----

* All names and page references are keyed to the Select Bibliography, which follows.

poets, primarily from Ovid, to tell typically medieval stories
(i.e. *Pamphilus* and *Babio*). In all cases the combination of old
and new results in giving "hybrid vigor" to the medieval com-
positions. The best of these works have an energy and a charm
which are wholly their own.

The first thing that may strike the reader of the works in
this volume is their bawdiness. The sexual explicitness is even
more surprising since the authors were clerics, men educated
by the Church. At least one, William of Blois, was a member
of the Church establishment; he was abbot of a monastery in
Sicily at the time he wrote his racy *Alda.* A previous genera-
tion of scholars was shocked by the more obscene passages (for
examples, see below), but if we disregard the sexual explicitness of *Alda, Lidia,* and other such works, we blind ourselves
to one of the most interesting issues. *Alda* is frankly a dirty
story, and as such it is far from isolated in medieval Latin literature. Latin erotic literature of the twelfth century is often
more elaborately pornographic and explicitly sensual than contemporary vernacular writing. The vernacular parallels which
immediately come to mind — the fabliaux, the allegorical but
graphic rape at the end of the *Romance of the Rose,* Boccaccio's
bawdy stories, or a few of the *Canterbury Tales* — were composed one or two centuries later. Were the Latin works, then,
merely the products of precocious and prurient clerics?

Secular Latin literature is often a form of avant-garde or
"underground" literature. The men who wrote it, though most
remain anonymous, were not necessarily the *vagantes,* the
dropouts from ecclesiastical culture. Some, like William of
Blois and Arnulf of Orléans (or, among lyric poets, Serlo of
Wilton), were men of great learning and high position. Their
erotic works, moreover, were not meant for the general public
but for a well-educated, sophisticated audience, connoisseurs of
Ovid and Terence. Such men knew by heart Horace's famous
dictum that poets "wish either to profit or to delight" (*Art of
Poetry* 333; see Suchomski, pp. 99-157; Hunt, "Prodesse,"
1979). Official medieval poetic doctrine (and indeed some
modern criticism as well) tended to interpret Horace's "either
... or" to mean "both ... and"; and critics, medieval and

modern, have been quick to point out the edifying lessons to be learned from a work, and to condemn out of hand something which could not bear an explicitly moral interpretation (Peter of Blois' comments on his brother's *Alda,* cited below, are typical of the "official" attitude). In private, however, clerics, or some of them, might be less insistent in their demand for moral edification. A work like *Alda* is very funny, and that alone justifies, and explains, its existence.

Nonetheless William of Blois and the others remained conventional clerics. These comedies, like much Latin erotic literature, verge on the satiric, sometimes on the misogynistic (see the studies of Haller and Schotter). They belong to what Northrop Frye has called the "ironic mode" (p. 34), in which the hero is viewed from above. The reader (or audience) feels superior to him and observes his foibles with detached amusement. These authors wrote to titillate, not to corrupt. They are not saying, "Go thou and do likewise," but, "Lord, what fools these mortals be!"

The commonest topic of scholarly discussion concerning the Latin "elegiac comedies," as the quotation marks often employed indicate, is their genre. Even though many of the works are designated in manuscripts as *comoedia,* most scholars have argued against too literal an interpretation of the word. But if the consensus of scholarly opinion holds that the works are not comedies, there is less agreement on what they actually are. Brondsted, for example, tracing the debt owed by the texts to classical sources, claims that the "medieval Comedia was originally and basically designed as the vehicle of lyrical complaint whether blended with amorous material or not" (p. 268). This line of reasoning emphasizes the importance of Ovid over that of Terence, and points to the evident use made by the medieval poets not only of the *Art of Love* and the *Amores* but also of the *Heroides.* Certainly the complaint plays a large role in *Pamphilus, Babio,* and above all in the *Aulularia,* whose principal character is named Querulus ("Complainer"). Such a definition, however, fails to account for many aspects of the works in question, and it does not really advance our knowledge of the genre.

The two authors whose influence is most plain are Ovid and Terence, but scholars are in doubt as to how to interpret that fact (on Terence, see Pittaluga, 1982). Plautus in the Middle Ages was far less familiar and may not have been directly read, although, as Bate (1979, p. 4) has pointed out, at least one member of the Palatine family of Plautine manuscripts was known in central France in the ninth or tenth century (see Lindsay, *Captivi*, p. 1). Perhaps swayed by the sexual nature of much of the humor, Edmond Faral emphatically maintained that the works were better considered Latin fabliaux than genuinely theatrical plays ("Le fabliau," 1924, p. 321); Ian Thompson prefers the rubric "Latin comic tales" (p. 53). While Faral believed that the French fabliaux were derived from the Latin texts, later scholars have not concurred and generally content themselves with pointing to analogies between the two. This view has a certain validity in that there are interesting similarities between the two groups of texts.

Studies devoted to the Old French fabliaux can illuminate some of the thematic concerns of the Latin "comedies," without, however, suggesting that the Latin works are necessarily, or only, fabliaux as narrowly defined. In a recent article on the principles of fabliau structure, Roy J. Pearcy explores "the proposition that the comic action of the fabliaux is based on a concern with epistemology, and with the failure of the characters to perceive data correctly" (p. 68). Pearcy does not consider the Latin texts, defining fabliaux strictly as French verse tales, nor does he suggest that the fabliaux poets had any "theoretical interest" in abstract philosophical problems. But the Latin poets may have had some such concerns. Certainly a work like the *Geta* fits well into his scheme, and *Lidia* and the *Aulularia* deal extensively with the discrepancy between perception and reality.

Gregg Lacy, writing of the Old French tales, maintains that they "derive at least part of their humor through certain stylistic allusions to the *gravis stylus*" (p. 353). In a similar vein, the Latin works reveal a delight in consciously inflated language, often mistaken or misapplied. The rustic Babio's attempts to imitate courtly rhetoric fail in most humorous ways, as, for example, in the amusing scene in which his desire to be rid of his rival Croceus causes him to make "Freudian slips" in his speech of welcome. To take this point further, both the comedies and the fabliaux, as Stephen L. Wailes suggests, are concerned to depict "the playing of roles by actors unsuited to them, specifically the enacting by socially inferior persons of parts appropriate to higher classes. It is a technique of parody in the strict sense of the word — the distorting imitation of a known model for the sake of humor" (p. 640). The Latin works frequently portray inadequate role-players — the silly fool Geta, for instance, trying to imitate the language of the philosophical schools, or the rustic and stingy Babio trying to sound like the noble and generous hero of courtly romance. Pamphilus, who by his own admission has to work for his living, is represented as wealthy. All three would-be gentlemen ultimately prove unequal to the roles they attempt to play, and much of the humor derives from our perception of their failures. Such works contain large doses of satire. Significantly, in the Middle Ages, satire was considered a form of comedy. Horace and Persius were both called comic poets (Alain de Lille, *PL* 210, col. 115), and at least one famous medieval satire, the Archpoet's "Confession," is labeled a *comedia* in the *incipit* of some manuscripts.

Such arguments, which involve thematic affinities, do not preclude the possibility of a more genuinely dramatic nature for some of the works, particularly for *Babio* and *Pamphilus*. Gustave Cohen, the general editor of the two volumes in which fifteen of the so-called *Comediae* were first published as a corpus, argued for the true theatricality of the works, but he has been without many followers; indeed, fourteen of the editors of individual works in that series differed from him (Roy, p. 258). One problem is that, although first Cohen and now Ferruccio Bertini and his associates at Genoa have published the "Comedies" together as if they were a genuine collection, the works are not all an identical type of tale (Bertini, 1979; Hunt, 1978, p. 126). Hence they do not fit comfortably into a single generic pigeon-hole. *Pamphilus* and *Babio* may well be genuine drama; *Geta*, the *Aulularia*, and perhaps *Alda* are better viewed as mime, while the *Three Girls* and *Lidia* may indeed be "Latin comic tales," which, if performed, were most likely presented by a single person (see, however, the note to *Lidia* 226).

We have already noted Faral's emphatic opinion of the appropriate genre. Others have been inclined to view the works as mere literary exercises, quite independent of any form of drama (Sticca, p. 114). If generic questions are raised at all by these scholars, the "plays" are considered a branch of rhetoric. In this connection it is interesting to note that one, a brief narrative entitled *The Three Companions (De Tribus Sociis)*, is cited as an illustration of comic style in Geoffrey of Vinsauf's rhetorical treatise, *Poetria Nova* (lines 1888 ff.). Ian Thompson, for example, roundly discounts the possibility of drama: "'Comedy' normally implies a play with dialogue and no narrative, and no ancient drama would ever have been written in elegiacs. Moreover, none of them, except for *Babio*, is even remotely like a drama in form" (pp. 52-53). He then goes on to analyze the works' evident delight in learned puns and rhetoric. But word-play, rhetoric, and "comedy" are not necessarily mutually exclusive. Thompson is here guilty of applying to his evidence criteria that are excessively rigid and possibly anachronistic. While classical playwrights did not utilize the elegiac couplet (the preferred meter of the favorite medieval authority on things amatory, Ovid), medieval theoreticians such as John of Garland considered the meter appropriate to "comedy," however that term be defined, as he wrote: "all comedy is elegy, but the reverse is not true" (ed. Faral, *Les Arts poétiques*, 1924, p. 59). It is doubtful that even the most skillful medieval metrician could have managed the complicated quantitative meters of Plautus and Terence, actually thought in the Middle Ages to be prose, while the elegiac couplet is comparatively easy to imitate. Besides, two works contain no third-person narrative at all: the short *The Clerics and the Churl (De Clericis et Rustico*, not included in this volume) and *Babio*, for which Axton demonstrates "the play's dependence on a living tradition of performance" (p. 29; see also Vinay, p. 209, and Brennan, *passim*). The very popular *Pamphilus* contains only a half-line of narrative (71), and in *all other respects* closely "resembles a play in form." Since the gloss of Arnulf of Orléans (see below) mentions only three characters in *Pamphilus*, Dronke (1979) has ingeniously proposed taking this half-line as a comment by Pamphilus to himself; hence Venus' long speech becomes a form of interior monologue. Parallels for the inclusion of narrative lines in a dialogued work can also be found in vernacular drama; Cohen points out that the thirteenth- or fourteenth-century *Passion of Autun* contains narrative lines which are awkward if that work were "acted" but create no difficulty in a mimed performance (p. XII). Perhaps the most persuasive evidence is that of Bruno Roy, who shows that Arnulf of Orléans, active around 1175 and probably himself a writer of comedy (see the introduction to *Lidia*), considered *Pamphilus* a stage play. Finally, works like *Geta*, the *Aulularia*, *Alda*, and *Pamphilus* are usually assigned to the period (ca. 1140-1170) to which date the first developed Latin religious drama — the two *Daniel* plays (ca. 1140 and 1175), Hildegard of Bingen's *Ordo Virtutum* (ca. 1155), the Tegernsee *Play of Antichrist* (ca. 1160), and the Montecassino *Passion* (1160). (For further discussion see the various studies of Bate, Bertini, and Dronke, 1979.)

It used to be argued that there was no such thing as genuinely dramatic comedy in the Middle Ages. In a study concentrating on the literary evidence prior to the year 1100, however, Ogilvy writes that "the old notion that mediaeval scholars did not recognize comedy as a dramatic form should have been pretty well exploded" (pp. 617-18). Axton and Brennan have examined the evidence for the theatricality of *Babio*. *Pamphilus* as well bears many imprints of a work intended as representational drama. It contains an elaborate eavesdropping scene in which the bawd's praises of Pamphilus' merits for Galathea's benefit gains in humor if we *see* the girl's reactions. There are similar scenes in *Babio*, *Geta*, and the *Aulularia*. Unlike the religious dramas, neither *Babio* nor *Pamphilus* contains explicit stage directions, but there are numerous internal hints of what characters are to be doing. (It should be noted that the dramas of Plautus and Terence are also free of external stage directions.) When Pamphilus, for example, first sees Galathea approaching, he determines to speak to her even though he says that he knows his voice will

tremble; such a line tells the actor how to interpret the following speech. Pamphilus announces that Galathea is beautiful
and that her hair is uncovered but there is no other description
of the heroine, a most unusual situation if the work is considered to be merely a branch of rhetoric since the rhetorical
handbooks are filled with instructions on the proper techniques
of description. In this respect, contrast the long description in
The Three Girls (33-56). *Babio* also lacks such descriptive passages. Furthermore, in *Pamphilus* whenever one character is
supposed to change location, the formula *convenit ire* ("I must
go") appears, and on several occasions the author has conveniently provided crossing speeches, words for a character to
speak as he or she goes from one place to another; lines
281-84 are a good example (Vinay, p. 252, discusses lines
339-54 in this context).

But if works such as *Babio* and *Pamphilus* may be conceived of as drama in conventional terms, what of a work such
as *Geta*, which contains far too many narrative lines for us to
argue for an *acted* version, roughly one-fifth of the work? On
the other hand, there are numerous occasions where the action
is difficult to follow if we consider the work intended for reading only. Axton makes the same point in arguing for the theatricality of *Babio*: "It is hard to see why the author of *Babio*
should have gone to the trouble of reconstructing the conditions
of live performance so minutely as to make the text difficult for
private reading if public performance had not been his intention" (p. 29). In *Geta*, as in *Babio*, it is often hard to know who
is speaking, and for the sake of clarity in the translation I
have had at times to insert the speaker's name in square
brackets, even though the manuscript contains no such rubric.
If some dramatic form of representation were intended, these
difficulties would disappear. We could then *see* who was speaking. The work, furthermore, is replete with the visual techniques of drama. If the author did not have in mind some form of
physical mimesis for his work, he was nevertheless so familiar
with theatrical conventions that he introduced them gratui-
tously — a fact which argues for an active tradition of living
theater. In this regard eavesdropping scenes and the use of
asides are particularly significant (see Brennan, pp. 26-27, for

asides in *Babio*).

Of *Geta* and the *Aulularia*, however, even so staunch an advocate of theatrical performances in the Middle Ages as Benjamin Hunningher has written, "It is possible that the Latin works of ... Vitalis of Blois ... just as the *comoedia elegiaca*, owe something to the mimes, particularly in their themes, but they were in all probability intended as literary excursions of and for an intellectual group only, and can therefore hardly be included in a list of secular theatrical work" (p. 82, n. 46). Hunningher was, I believe, on the right track, but the debt to the mimes may be far greater than he was willing to concede, and it includes techniques as well as themes. First, if *Geta* and works like it were written "for an intellectual group only," that particular group was a numerous and influential one (for the possible relationship of William of Blois to the court of Henry II, see Bate, 1979). Secondly, while clerics may technically be considered members of a religious, not a secular, society, such a distinction is not particularly meaningful in this instance, or in many others: medieval popular and clerical culture were not always polar opposites (see Hunt, 1978, p. 121). The "religious" clerics penned many works whose position in the history of *secular* literature is unquestioned, works such as the *Waltharius*, the *Ruodlieb*, and the love poems of the *Carmina Burana* and other anthologies.

I would suggest that works like *Geta*, in spite of their learned language and erudite jokes, belong most closely to that popular and therefore largely ephemeral genre, the mime (Axton, p. 30, notes the appropriateness of *Babio* for mimed performance). While we have little evidence for literary comedy after Plautus and Terence, there are no signs that the mimes diminished in popularity. Hunningher writes, "The Roman stage was ruled by the mime" (p. 63). The persistence of the mimes is not attested by texts, for there are practically none extant from *any* period, but it is well documented by the Church's repeated strictures against theatrical shows and warnings against the evils presented by the performers, the *joculatores*, *histriones*, *mimi*, *saltatores* "jongleurs, actors, mimes, dancers." St. Augustine refers in his *Confessions*

(1.16.25) to having witnessed a performance, presumably by a
mime, of Jupiter's adulterous affairs: an *Amphrityron*, by any
chance? We cannot, moreover, dismiss the performers as
merely jugglers and acrobats, owners of dancing bears and the
like; there is good evidence, such as that provided by St.
Augustine, that they engaged in representational drama as
well. The most frequently cited condemnation of actors is that
of Isidore of Seville (*Etymologiae* 18.48), who defines *histriones*
as "actors ... who in women's clothing express the gestures of
unchaste women; there are others, moreover, who in their
dancing represent histories and [heroic] deeds." The depiction
of "histories and [heroic] deeds" implies a plot. Furthermore,
"dancing" does not mean "dance" as that term is used today,
but mime. The gloss of Arnulf of Orléans which mentions
Pamphilus refers to a musical performance in which the characters are described as dancing, miming; the verb is *saltantur*,
literally "leaping," the same verb used by Isidore, which
Arnulf carefully explains as "they represent by dances (*salta-
tiones*) and gestures" (Roy, p. 260).

Not all the "comedies," however, are equally dramatic.
There are significant stylistic differences between *Geta*, for
example, and *The Three Girls* or the highly rhetorical *Lidia*. In
these latter works, the poets sought elaborately varied meth-
ods of introducing the speeches, and they included adverbial
modification to help the reader visualize the action, using such
phrases as "she speaks flatteringly" (*blande profatur*, *Lidia*,
60), or "smiling tenderly at me [she] replied" (*Three Girls*,
147). Such interpretive comments are lacking, for example, in
Geta, where Vitalis relied on simple verbs like "says" and
"shouts."

In spite of the absence of scenarios, we know something
about the mimes' dramatic practices. The most celebrated
description of a mime's performance is a text, probably dating
to the Carolingian period, that purports to be the epitaph of the
mime Vitalis (not to be confused with our Vitalis of Blois):

I used to mimic the face, manner and words of
those talking, so that you would think many

people spoke from one mouth. The subject, presented with a twin image of himself before his eyes, would tremble to see a more real self existing in my faces. Oh, how often a lady saw herself in my performance, and blushed for shame, horribly embarrassed. Thus as many human forms as were seen in my body were snatched away with me by the dismal day of death" (trans. Axton, p. 17).

Such performances, however, did not escape the notice of the religious authorities. The Church's strictures against various types of theatrical performance were harsh; judging by the frequency with which they had to be repeated, they were also ineffectual. To give examples from a single century, Councils in 813, 816, 829, 847, and 890 all fulminated against the pernicious influence of mimes, and still more vehemently against those churchmen who displayed too great a fondness for such agents of the devil.

The origin of the licentious mimes is disputed (see the discussion of Nicoll). They appear to have been the descendants of the Greek *Phlyakes* (for which Greek vase paintings form our chief but convenient evidence) and the Latin *Atellanes*. One of the principal properties of the *Phlyakes*, if we may judge from the vase paintings, was a large phallus (Hunnigher provides a good series of illustrations), a property required for *Geta* (two of them, in fact, one for Geta and one for Archas), for *Babio*, and probably also for the "tail scene" in *Alda*. Condemnations of activities of the mimes constantly mentioned the unchaste nature of their performances (witness the lady's blushes mentioned by the epitaph of Vitalis and the quotation from Isidore of Seville, cited above).

Two points remain. It has often been observed that in the Middle Ages, although Terence was read widely, people had lost sight of the genuinely dramatic nature of his works; instead of seeing actors speaking on a stage, they imagined a reader, often thought to be sitting in a booth, who read the text aloud while mimes recreated the action. The evidence for this view is collected by Mary Hatch Marshall ("Theatre," 1950; see also the work of Jones and Morey on illustrated Terence manuscripts). The classic illustration is the so-called "Terence of the Dukes" from the Bibliothèque de l'Arsenal, Paris. The epitaph of Vitalis shows the pride a professional took in his ability to mimic the voices of both men and women. While this view of Terence and the performance techniques of ancient comedy was probably less universally held than has been thought (Marshall, "Boethius' Definition," 1950), it is largely valid. But such a method, utilizing the services of reader and mimes, would suit admirably the representational require-ments of such texts as *Geta* or the *Aulularia*.

The fact that the comedies are in Latin and popular per-formers such as the mimes were ignorant of that learned tongue seems to argue against my thesis. An observation like Hunningher's above on the intellectual nature of the audience points to such a view. Yet there is scattered evidence for pro-fessional actors performing Latin works. The first is admit-tedly controversial; the St. Martial *Troparium* depicts what appear to be secular actors performing the texts (Hunningher reproduces the illuminations). We have, moreover, a text which places the *Cambridge Songs*, Latin poems many of which are decidedly profane in nature, undisputably in the repertory of a jongleur; the satires of Sextus Amaricius Gallus mentions a performance of Poems 22, 31, and 41. Further-more, for the "comedies," only the reader needed to know Latin well; the mimes did not, or they needed to know only enough to pick up their cues, not an impossibility for speakers of medieval Romance languages (for the probable mutual intel-ligibility of Latin and romance vernacular, see Wright). Arnulf of Orléans' gloss mentions zithers and lyres as "the instru-ments which plays in the theater demand" (Dronke, 1979, p. 227). The mimes could operate like dancers, working with a system of beats in time to music of some sort.

Should professional performers have been lacking, many clerics, even ordained priests, appear to have been sufficiently familiar with dramatic techniques to engage in amateur theat-ricals if they wished (Cohen thought that the actors must have been students). Peter Abelard sharply castigated those members of the clergy who, on feast days, filled their halls with actors and squandered the Church's patrimony upon such riff-raff (*PL* 178, cols. 1211-12). The Church councils, as we have seen, were particularly outspoken in their condemnation of participation by the clergy in drama, a sure sign that the offense was being committed (for texts, see Faral 1910 and Waddell). Aelred of Rievaulx's objection, written between 1141-42, to preachers who gave too histrionic sermons paints a vivid picture; such pulpit hams "with the gestures of actors use their whole body, contort their lips, twist and wiggle their shoulders, and ... respond to each note with gesticulations of their fingers" (*Speculum Charitatis*, *PL* 195, col. 571). Alain de Lille, in his *Compendium of the Art of Preaching*, cautioned in a more general fashion against sermons which were excessively theatrical and smacked of the mimes (*PL* 210, col. 112). Finally, in the year 1180 Giraldus Cambrensis found himself scandalized by the behavior of the monks at Canterbury. He dined at high table and there, in addition to the "multitude of dishes," he noted with disapproval "the excessive superfluity of the signs" which the monks, obedient to the letter if not the spirit of the law of silence, made to one another (*Autobiography*, p. 71):

> ... there were those, to whom these gifts were brought, offering their thanks, and all of them gesticulating with fingers, hands, and arms, and whistling to one another in lieu of speaking, all ... in a manner more free and frivolous than was seemly; so that Giraldus seemed to be seated at a stage-play or among actors and jesters.

The words translated as "stage-play" are *ludos scenicos;* the term *scena* was reserved for secular presentations and was not applied to sacred drama.

To summarize: (1) Throughout the entire Middle Ages, from before the fall of Rome until well after the twelfth century, there is evidence for theatrical performances of some sort, and especially for mimes. Finding such performers utterly reprehensible, the Church constantly had to censure clerics who displayed too great a fondness for actors and their shows. (2) Terence was widely read, often in illustrated manuscripts which depicted actors; some illuminations show a reader and mimes. (3) Works in Latin do exist, some of them imitations of Terentian or Plautine originals in form and sometimes in content, which are well adapted to staging with reader and mimes. Therefore the best conclusion seems to be that some of the Latin "comedies" were intended to be presented, not merely read, for the titillation of audiences composed of clerics, students, or courtiers. Testimony like that of Peter Abelard cited above indicates that performances for the clergy could be financially rewarding. Unlike the vernacular mimes, however, the Latin texts have survived because their clever use of rhetoric, their debt to classical authors, and their parody of the schools endeared them to those with the means of preservation at their disposal, the clerical scribes. The actors could have been professionals who knew Latin, perhaps those notorious "ribald clerics," the *vagantes*, sometimes called "Goliards"; they could equally well have been amateurs, students or other clerics who had seen profane actors plying their trade and who decided to try their luck at acting or miming, perhaps on one of those feast days when, Abelard complained, even prelates were wont to indulge their taste for theatrical shows.

PAMPHILUS

The most popular, and the most important, of the Latin comedies is *Pamphilus*, an anonymous work probably written in France at some time during the twelfth century. It is usually assigned to the middle of the century (Blumenthal), but recently Peter Dronke (1979) has convincingly argued for a date closer to 1100. A citation of Venus's line 71 — "labor improbus omnia vincit" ("Bold and persistent labor conquers all") — by John of Salisbury gives a *terminus post quem* of 1159 (Hunt, 1978, pp. 130-31). The work was so popular that it circulated in little manuscript "pamphlets," a word which is in fact derived from the title of the play (Morawski, p. 14, n. 1).

Pamphilus is in some ways a puzzling work, and it raises a number of issues central to any study of the Latin comedies. These include its genre, its author's intention, and its influence. I have already discussed genre. I believe that the work is a genuine drama, a hypothesis which was put to the test in 1974 when I first translated *Pamphilus* for a staged production, utilizing the services of four readers and four mimes. The production, staged for the meeting of the Medieval Association of the Pacific, was admirably directed by Robert A. Potter of the Department of Dramatic Art, University of California, Santa Barbara. The present translation, based on the text of Evesque but taking into account the more recent critical edition of Pittaluga (1980), derives from that performance. As a result, the rendition is somewhat freer than are those of the other plays. The final criterion was that an actor had to be able to speak the lines and an audience to understand them. If the proof of the pudding lies in the eating, *Pamphilus* is a dramatic work. The production was well received by scholars and students alike. A clever mime can make what seems dull on the printed page into a theatrical tour de force (Venus's long speech of advice, 71-144, is a case in point). A good bawd will steal the show.

In the manuscripts the work is generally entitled *Pamphilus de amore* ("Pamphilus on love"), and for a time the work was taken to be an autobiography written by Pamphilus himself, a fact which may have contributed to its popularity in the Middle Ages (see Rico, pp. 308-309; also Spitzer). Unlike most other works in this collection, it is not called a comedy but a book *(liber;* Rico, p. 309), an argument which would seem to damage my contention that the work is drama. The dramatic *Babio*, however, is also catagorized as a *liber* in the Digby manuscript (Brennan, p. 96). If we do not consider the ending of *Pamphilus* happy, this objection may not be a serious one.

Although the work is fiction, not autobiography, it is about the nature of love, as the manuscript title indicates. The name

"Pamphilus" means "all love" or "wholly in love." Two characters in Terence's dramas were named Pamphilus (in the
Hecyra and the *Andria),* as was a "feigned lover" *(fictus
amans)* in the ninth-century debate *Terentius et Delusor.* But if
the name is old, the story is original, although the work's debt
to classical authors, primarily Ovid to whom the work was
ascribed in some manuscripts, is great. Venus' speech of
advice to Pamphilus is taken almost verbatim from *The Art of
Love,* Book 1, and there are many other echoes of the classical
poet throughout. But how are we to take the lover's rape of
Galathea? Is the girl merely a medieval reincarnation of
Ovid's sophisticated Corinna, who in *Amores* 1.5 enjoyed losing
the struggle with Ovid to retain her tunic?

In the *Art of Love* (1.669-74) Ovid had written:

> oscula qui sumpsit, si non et cetera sumit,
>   haec quoque, quae data sunt, perdere dignus erit.
> quantum defuerat pleno post oscula uoto?
>   ei mihi, rusticitas, non pudor ille fuit.
> uim licet appelles: grata est uis ista puellis;
>   quod iuuat, inuitae saepe dedisse uolunt.

> Whoever has taken kisses, if he does not take the
> rest, deserves to lose even those things which had
> been granted. After kisses, how much was miss-
> ing from your entire desire? Alas, it was lack of
> sophistication, not modesty! You may call it vio-
> lence if you wish; this form of violence is pleasing
> to girls; women often wish to give "unwillingly"
> that which they want to give.

Was Galathea, in accord with Ovidian teaching, merely saying
"no" when she meant "yes"? The author of the medieval introduction (or *accessus)* to the work apparently thought so, as he
considered the "utility" of *Pamphilus* to be the fact that, having read it, each man could know how to find a beautiful girl
for himself. In 1344 the Chancellor of Oxford University ban-
ned the work along with the *Art of Love* "or any other other
book which would seduce or provoke the students to vice"

(Anstey, p. 441). I think, nevertheless, that the author's purpose was rather different, and it is one which reveals an interest in feminine psychology (see Vinay, p. 267; Bertini, 1979, p. 74), and a sensitivity worthy of Ovid himself (see Curran), and which are close to unique in medieval Latin literature. *Pamphilus* is an attempt to apply Ovid's precepts, the "Comandemanz d'Ovide," to real people and to see what happens. It is my contention that Galathea was not dissimulating. She was a young virgin, not a courtesan, and she did not want to be raped.

The author of *Pamphilus* has adopted the clear-eyed, unsentimental Ovidian stance; he has perceived Ovid's urbane cynicism, and, like Ovid, enjoyed exposing the gap between word and deed (see Elliott, 1981 and 1982). The opening line of Venus' speech of Ovidian advice on how to succeed in love is not from Ovid but from Vergil, a slight variation of *Georgics* 1.145-46 "Labor vicit omnia improbus," "Hard work has conquered all." The adjective *improbus*, however, means both "persistent" and "improper," while *labor* ("labor, work") connotes *hard* work ("drudgery"). The author of *Pamphilus* has adopted *labor*, coupled with *ars* (which means both "art" and "skill, craft, guile"), as thematic words for his work; *labor*, for example, occurs eleven times in the *Art of Love*, thirty-four times in the *Georgics*, and twenty-seven times in the 780 lines of *Pamphilus*. The young lover wanted Venus to *give* him the girl; the goddess suggested *labor* instead. This is an essentially unromantic, rather cynical view of love, requiring a combination of hard work and skillful deceit (*ars*).

In many ways Pamphilus appears to be the stereotypical Ovidian or courtly lover: he turns pale (cf. the *Art of Love* 1.729, "Let every lover turn pale"), grows weak in the knees at the sight of his beloved, forgets the speech he had worked out, and so forth. His has been an "amour de loin," as he maintains that he has loved Galathea for three years without daring to speak to her. He claims, moreover, that all he wants are the first four of the five "grades" of love — sight, conversation, kisses, and embraces (the fifth is the "act"; see Friedman). His behavior, up to a crucial point, is identical with that of almost any other lover in courtly romance. Unlike the average romance hero, however, the first time that Pamphilus is alone with the girl in private, he abandons his courtly phrases and rapes her in spite of her repeated protests.

The figure of the go-between is perhaps the most important contribution of *Pamphilus* to medieval literature. While this character owes something to Dipsas, the old bawd of *Amores* 1.8, she is much more developed in the medieval work, and her descendants are legion — Lusca in *Lidia,* the old nurse in *Alda,* La Vieille of the *Romance of the Rose,* and Trotaconventos in the *Libro de Buen Amor,* to give only four obvious examples. She is untrustworthy, mercenary, and ready to lie cheerfully to both Pamphilus and Galathea in order to increase their indebtedness to her. She has the last word in this "comedy," and her final words may strike us as black ones; having married off Pamphilus and Galathea (or so it seems), whether they wish it or no, she exhorts them, "Never forget me!" (780). Since all talk of marriage has in fact originated with her (Pittaluga, 1982, p. 298), we may wonder how happy this traditional happy ending will prove to be. But however we imagine the future condition of the hero and heroine, it is clear that the real winner in this drama is the self-interested, avaricious bawd.

The crux in interpreting *Pamphilus* is clearly whether or not Galathea was dissembling when she cried out for Pamphilus to take his hands off her. Venus had advised (129-33):

> And if doubtfully she hesitates, the ignorant girl,
> wondering whether she should do what you want,
> that's the moment to wear down her resistance with
> temptations,
> so that swiftly, victoriously, you can enjoy your love.
> A mind in doubt is swayed by a little hard labor.

Pamphilus forgot the temptations and relied on labor.

In the *Art of Love* Ovid was not talking about the seduction of virgins but about the games sophisticated people play

(*Amores* 1.5 makes plain exactly the kind of woman Ovid's Corinna was — an experienced courtesan). In *Pamphilus*, Galathea is young and inexperienced; she has to run home when she sees her parents returning from church. She has been well brought up and knows that being alone with a man is dangerous. In the play we see her gradually falling in love — not really with Pamphilus, for she hardly knows him and his first speech seems to make little impression on her, but with the idea of being in love, as the bawd skillfully manipulates her feelings by making claims for Pamphilus, many of which prove to be outright lies. Galathea was eager to be in love. Sexual intercourse, or rape, is a different matter.

Galathea protests continually during the rape scene, crying that Pamphilus is hurting her. He has to restrain her hands. At the end, she declares (695-96):

> You've conquered me, however strongly I resisted,
> but all hope of love is shattered between us — forever!

But Pamphilus, panting from his exertions, does not appear to hear her words. He does observe that she refuses to look at him and continues to cry (note the use of "internal stage directions" in these lines). At first he seems ready to accept the blame for what he has done but then contrives to shift it to *her* — it was all her fault; her beauty tempted him. (The notion that the fault is the rape-victim's, perpetuated by Freud, is not a new one; see Albin). When the bawd asks Galathea what has happened, the girl is furious. She compares herself to a series of victims — to animals (a hare, a fish, a bird) caught by hungry predators — and she imagines that her parents will throw her out of the house. While the work has no explicit stage directions or narrative comments to guide our interpretation, Galathea's continued tears and the imagery she uses suggest that she is not pretending. There is, after all, a difference between seduction and rape.

It here becomes important that *Pamphilus* is dramatic, because the audience's form of identification with the protagonists differs for drama and for a "comic tale." Drama takes as

its opening premise that we are watching "real" people on the
stage; the point of *Pamphilus* is that someone may get hurt
when Ovidian love, all well and good if it remains confined to
books, is applied to real people. Galathea did not like being
raped, and continued to cry. The bawd proposed that marriage
will solve everything, but we may wonder what sort of a marriage it would be. It is perhaps not irrelevant to note that it
was during the twelfth century (in 1140 to be precise) when
the doctrine of consent in marriage assumed special importance for canonists such as Gratian and when it was maintained that a woman need not marry the man who raped her
(see Noonan).

Pamphilus stands in the mainstream of twelfth-century literature. Not only was it widely read, but it deals with many
issues prominent in the thought of the century. The vernacular
texts concerning love may be better known than the Latin, but
both Latin and vernacular authors were concerned with many
of the same issues. Much, for example, has been written about
the phenomenon now known as "courtly love." In exceeding the
wishes of his beloved, Pamphilus violated one of the "rules" of
courtly love (Andreas Capellanus, Dialogue Five, Rule Twelve;
ed. Parry, p. 82). Until the date of composition can be determined with absolute certainty, the position of *Pamphilus* in the
history of the amatory literature of the twelfth century
remains vexed. If, as seems likely, Dronke's dating of the work
to the beginning of the twelfth century is correct, then it may
be one of the seminal works of the period. It is, in any event, a
major document in the history of "courtoisie" but a sceptical
one. It exposes to the light of day the gap between the words
and the deeds of enthusiastic lovers, and highlights the risk of
violence which may accompany unrestrained love. Passion is
dangerous.

My interpretation of *Pamphilus* is a serious one. It sets
the work somewhat apart from the others contained in this
volume. Whatever the correct interpretation of the work and
its genre, *Pamphilus* was enormously popular; indeed it is
impossible in a short space to do full justice to the subject of
the work's influence. Garbáty goes so far as to state that it

was "recognized and quoted by almost every man of learning from the Middle Ages to the Renaissance" (1967, p. 457). Becker's critical edition recognizes some 170 manuscripts. According to Dronke (1979, pp. 225-26), the introduction, or *accessus*, to *Pamphilus* (printed by Huygens, p. 53), was written close to the middle of the twelfth century, a fact which demonstrates the work's status as a "classic" by that date. By the end of the twelfth or the beginning of the thirteenth century, the play formed part of the jongleur repertory (presumably in Provençal), for Guiraut de Calanson in his *ensenhamen*, "Fadet joglar," castigates a performer for not knowing it (Pirot, pp. 253-54). It was translated, or better, adapted, into Old French by Jehan Brasdefer around 1225, and was also translated into the Venetian dialect around 1250 and into Old Norse some time in the thirteenth century. It was one of the sources for the *Romance of the Rose* and was familiar to Chaucer and Boccaccio (see the bibliography; in Boccaccio's *Fiammetta* the seducer is named Panfilo). But the work's greatest success was probably in Spain, where Juan Ruiz modeled his bawd Trotaconventos in the *Libro de Buen Amor* directly on the bawd in *Pamphilus*, as well as retelling the story (Seidenspinner), and the Latin work served as the model for the *Celestina* (Lida). Pamphilus was listed by Hugh of Trimberg in 1280 in his list of books every gentleman should read. By 1610 there were sixteen printed editions. The first, by Jean Prot, was in print by 1470 — one year before the *editio princeps* of Ovid.

GETA
By Vitalis of Blois

Geta, a very free adaptation of Plautus' *Amphitryon*, is one of the earliest and most successful of the medieval Latin comedies. All we know of its author, Vitalis of Blois, is that he was a cleric, for only a cleric would have had the education and the motivation to write a Latin adaptation of Plautus, satirizing the growing craze for philosophical studies; and that he was the author of two Latin comedies, for in the prologue to the *Aulularia* Vitalis names himself as the author of these two works. Bertini (1980) favors the period 1125-1130 for the composition of *Geta*. The work's success was enormous and immediate; the many surviving manuscripts (at least 66, and some 17 are known to have been lost; Bertini, 1979, p. 71) offer eloquent testimony to its popularity, as do the numerous citations in the *florilegia* and in the works of other writers. It may have influenced Chrétien de Troyes (Hunt, 1978). At the end of the fourteenth century, it was translated into Italian, and around 1420 Eustache Deschamps translated it into French (for details, see Bertini's edition, pp. 151-59).

After a summarizing "argument," the work opens with a prologue spoken by the author in which he defends himself and deplores the literary mores of the day. In this respect it resembles the plays of Terence rather than Plautus, for in the Plautine *Amphitryon* the prologue is spoken by Mercury, who fills the audience in on the action up to the return of Amphitryon, with which the play begins. While *Geta* tells the same basic story as does Plautus' play — Jupiter's seduction of Amphitryon's wife and the ensuing confusion caused by the double cast of characters — the similarity stops there. Vitalis alters names: Sosia becomes Geta, Mercury is called Archas, a post-classical name for the god. The medieval work makes no mention of the celebrated child, the hero Hercules, who resulted from the god's dalliance. Amphitryon himself is demoted from commander-in-chief of the Theban army to impoverished philosophy student, returning laden with books, not spoils of war, and is even displaced from his role as the protagonist of the play by his foolish servant Geta. Amphitryon becomes a minor character who appears only in the last section of the work, while the servants, Geta and Birria, together with Geta's double, Archas, steal the show. Such changes in detail and emphasis may be intentional (Bate, 1976, p. 7) or they may be ascribed to Vitalis' reliance upon an intermediate source (Bertini, 1980).

Vitalis, like most of the other identifiable authors of the Latin comedies, appears to have come from the Loire Valley, an area famous for the study of classical literature. There was, moreover, considerable hostility between the traditional schools (such as Orléans) oriented towards grammar and literary studies, and Paris, whose specialty was the new dialectic. A stellar lecturer like Peter Abelard had attracted students to Paris by droves, and that city was soon to eclipse all competition. In *Geta*, however, Parisian studies provided a ready subject for satire.

Although *Geta* derives a certain amount of its humor from the favorite fabliau themes of sexual innuendo and misconduct, most of the jokes are at the expense of philosophy, not sex. The real target, however, is probably not logic in general but more specifically those who try to practice that complicated art without sufficient knowledge or skill. In the *Metalogicon* (3.17, p. 117), completed in 1159 and therefore roughly contemporary with *Geta*, John of Salisbury complained of precisely those students who declaimed without full command of the complexities of their subject, "attempting to explain, contrary to the intention of the author [Aristotle], what is really a most profound question, and a matter [that should be reserved] for more advanced studies." Logic, as Birria (a wise fool) remarks, can convert an ordinary fool (Geta) into a madman (453; see also Hunt, "Aristotle," 1979, p. 124).

The remarks of Wailes, cited above, on role-playing in the *comoedia* and fabliaux are particularly relevant here. Geta had accompanied Amphitryon to "Athens" (Paris was known as "the Athens of the North" [Bate, 1976, p. 5]); he apes the philosophical jargon of the schools but bungles it. Boasting, for example, of the amazing sophistry he has learned by which he can prove that man is an ass (164), he in turn is convinced by equally specious reasoning that he himself is nothing, not even an ass (one was supposed to prove the *difference* between Socrates, or man in general, and an ass; the joke reappears in *Babio*). There are many examples of this use, or misuse, of logic for humorous effect. But while most of the jokes are general, at the expense of all inept practitioners, some may be more specific.

One of the major subjects parodied in *Geta* is the problem of universals. While medieval philosophy did to some extent

concern itself with other issues, prior to the contributions of
Avicenna and Averroes and the rediscovery of most of Aristotle, medieval philosophers had practically no other strictly
philosophical problem to discuss (Gilson, p. 153). Universals
were indeed heatedly discussed with the result that by the end
of the century the polemic excluded all other topics, leading
John of Salisbury, for one, to denounce the sterility of purely
dialectical thinking. (In the following discussion, my debt to
Etienne Gilson's *History of Christian Philosophy* is, to quote
Geta himself, tangible and therefore real.) In brief, the question of universals as raised by Porphyry involved the following
concerns: (1) Do universals exist in reality or only in thought?
(2) If they exist in reality, are they corporeal or incorporeal?
(3) Are they separate from sensible things or involved in them?
To these questions Peter Abelard added more. (1) What is
there which enables us to give things common names? (2) If
there are no such things as actually existing universals, what
do the common names designate? (3) If the particular things
signified by universals were destroyed, would their names still
have the same meaning?

Evidence of these all-compelling issues crops up throughout
Geta's muddled discourse. I give only two examples. (1) The
use of the terms *vox* and *nomen* (255-60, and throughout): *vox*
and *nomen* can mean both grammatical "voice" and "noun" as
well as speaking "voice" and "name." Furthermore, Roscelin,
Abelard's former teacher whom Abelard ridiculed, taught that
universals were *voces* "voices" while Abelard himself contended
that they were *nomina* "names." So we find Geta very concerned to know what his *name* will be if it is not Geta (402),
and he decides that he does in fact exist when Amphitryon
addresses him by the name "Geta" (437). (2) In his widely-
read commentary on Porphyry's *Isagoge* (*PL* 64, col. 114),
Boethius held that all individuals possess in common the
essence of their species but inevitably differ from one another
by a collection of "accidents" — details of color, size, shape of
nose, and so forth. Therefore poor Geta is wholly annihilated,
both philosophically and metaphorically, when he meets someone (Archas) who coincides with him in every "accident" (321
ff.; for further discussion see Bertini, 1979).

A few of the jokes may be aimed more directly at Abelard himself. Keith Bate (1976, p. 21) sees in the constant talk of "being a man" a reference to the celebrated "unmanning" of Abelard in 1119. In a similar vein, consider lines 409-410:

> Sic sum, sic non sum. Pereat dialectica per quam
> Sic perii penitus; nunc scio : scire nocet.

> Therefore I am; therefore I am not.
> Oh damnation to this dialectic
> which has condemned me utterly to non-existence.
> Now I have knowledge but knowledge is dangerous.

In the expression "Sic sum, sic non sum," Bate (1976, p. 20) notes a reference to Abelard's treatise *Sic et Non (Yes and No)*, compounded by an allusion to Abelard's disastrous tutoring of Heloise (*penitus* "wholly" being a pun on "penis" — and like all puns, a translator's despair). The reference to Abelard may be still more elaborate: Abelard's *Ethics* was subtitled "Scito te ipsum" "Know thyself"; the work, in circulation before 1139, aroused the vehement ire of Bernard of Clairvaux and his followers. Abelard and his teachings were condemned in 1140. Finally, that Abelard should be held up to ridicule by a comedy may in itself have point; in his *Christian Theology* (*PL* 178, cols. 1211-12) Abelard explicitly condemned those clerics too fond of actors and theatrical entertainments.

AULULARIA
By Vitalis of Blois

The *Aulularia* is the second comedy composed by Vitalis of Blois; in line 27 of the Prologue he names himself as the author of *Geta* as well. It did not, however, enjoy the great popularity of Vitalis' earlier endeavor, and with reason, for it lacks *Geta's* sparkle. While there are at least sixty manuscripts of *Geta*, there are only two of the *Aulularia*, plus a short fragment. After a detailed examination of the evidence, Ferruccio Bertini, whose edition forms the basis of this translation, concludes that the *Aulularia* was composed prior to 1145. Its model was not Plautus' play but an anonymous fourth- or fifth-century reworking called the *Querolus* (for the character's name I have kept the spelling "Querulus," found in the medieval manuscripts of the *Aulularia*, for the sake of the pun).

In general Vitalis' adaptation follows its late antique model fairly closely. Vitalis shortened the play, added the philosophical lore, and made other minor changes, one of which is particularly relevant to the question of genre. The work cannot be genuine drama, as there are too many narrative lines, some of which, for example, describe such undramatic events as the passage of time ("The seventh day brings the servant home," 285). This fact, however, does not preclude the possibility of a mimed performance (one can visualize Sardana ostentatiously walking in place during the line). An addition made by Vitalis suggests mimed performance even more strongly. One of the funniest moments in the medieval *Aulularia* is the carefully staged eavesdropping scene (383 ff.) in which Gnatho and Clinia whet Querulus' curiosity about "Paul," the newly-arrived magician. There is nothing which corresponds to this scene in the *Querolus*, as in that work the slave Sardanapallus (= Gnatho) simply tells Querolus about the arrival of the wonder-worker (ed. Ranstrand, p. 27). Much of the humor of an eavesdropping scene derives from its visual nature; without this advantage, it is a rather cumbersome and roundabout way to convey information. The solution of the *Querolus* is economical but lacks the wit of the *Aulularia*. Vitalis' alteration bespeaks an acquaintance with the stage in some form or other.

Like *Geta*, the *Aulularia* bears testimony to its author's interest in philosophy, for the text is replete with philosophical in-jokes. Instead of the references to nominalism and the universals, so much the concern in *Geta*, in the *Aulularia* the focus shifts to the physical and astronomical sciences (see the introduction to Bertini's edition, pp. 44-45), represented by such works as the *Hexaemeron* of Thierry of Chartres, the *De mundi universitate sive Megacosmus et Microcosmus* of Bernard Silvester, and the *Philosophia mundi* of William of Conches. In *Geta* the satiric drive had been directed against the Parisian schools; in this second work it appears to be aimed more at Chartres. The satire here, however, lacks the humor and verve of the lampoons of dialectic reasoning found in *Geta*. Querulus and his household Lar indulge in a lengthy and rather tedious discussion of Pythagorean and Platonic doctrine at the beginning of the play. The later remarks (649 ff.) about nature's abhorrence of a vacuum are somewhat funnier because they are directly related to the plot, but all in all it sounds more pedantic than comic.

As in *Geta*, much of the wit of the *Aulularia* derives from the elevated language of the philosophical schools being put in the mouths of fools and slaves who predictably bungle the complex terminology. For example, after attempting a pompous logical discourse on the nature of his misery, introduced by a pretentious *ergo* (79), in a moment of rare honesty Querulus lashes out against the difficulties of Platonic reasoning:

> I hate Plato's dreams woven of ambiguities,
> since he strove to sing things I can't understand.

Querulus, like Plautus' Euclio before him, is that stock figure of fun, the miser, and not a philosopher. He goes on to say that the only good thing in Platonic doctrine was the rejection of the vast Olympian pantheon. From Querulus' point of view, a multitude of gods calls for a multitude of expensive sacrifices.

The work is larded with quotations from classical authorities. To hear fools mangle them or use them inappropriately must have appealed to a medieval audience. As Marcel Girard, the editor of the work in Cohen's series, noted with apparent relief (p. 65), the work is free of the sexual humor which enlivens the other comedies (did this fact contribute to the relatively few extant copies of the work?). It is the only one of the comedies in which no woman appears, as both *Querolus* and Vitalis' reworking of it discarded the Plautine love plot.

BABIO

Although the other works in this volume (with the possible exception of *Pamphilus*) probably originated in France, *Babio* may come from England, as four of the five manuscripts are English, and the only authors to make reference to it, Robert Holkot and John Gower, were also English (Faral, 1948, pp. lviii-lix). There are, however, affinities with other French works to suggest that France is the country of origin. The distinction, moreover, is not particularly meaningful for the twelfth century, when intellectual exchange across the Channel was common (for discussion, see Brennan, pp. 3-5).

The usual arguments have been advanced concerning the correct genre to which the piece should be assigned. In his edition Faral predictably traced similarities with the fabliaux, while others, notably Brennan and Axton, have argued cogently for the genuinely dramatic nature of this work. There is no third-person narrative at all in *Babio* and there is much that appears theatrical, including the presence of walk-on parts — Croceus' gluttonous companions and Babio's associates. As Axton has shown (p. 30), the brief crossing of a trained dog would not strain the resources of a medieval troop of players, nor would the final castration scene. Brennan notes that the author has restricted time and place far more narrowly than is necessary for a non-dramatic piece (pp. 10-11; also 20-32). There is one more piece of evidence supporting this thesis. There are five major characters in *Babio:* Babio, his wife Petula, her daughter Viola, Viola's suitor Croceus, and the wily servant Fodius. The rhetorician, John of Garland, himself an Englishman, writing of "comedia perfecta," noted that such a work has five principal characters (*Parisiana Poetria*, p. 80, cited by Hunt, 1978, p. 122).

Nevertheless, in terms of themes, the affinities with fabliaux are evident. The plot conforms closely to the fabliau tale-type, "The Cuckold Beaten and Content" (Nykrog, p. 23n; a similar story is the well known fabliau *The Bourgeoise of Orléans).* Babio feigns a journey, returns in order to catch his wife in the act, but ends up being caught himself. If his "contentment" at the end is doubtful, from the point of view of Fodius and Petula the result is the same. He is *hors de combat*, and they are free to continue their sport.

The anonymous author makes much of his classical learning, and indeed much of the humor derives from a misuse of classical allusions (e.g. the false oaths by which Fodius deceives Babio, 271 ff.). As Axton remarks, *"Babio* is notable for its indecency and its grammar" (p. 29). Furthermore, when Babio inappropriately compares Viola to a series of women not necessarily known for fidelity — Phyllis, Thais, Helen, Corinna (36-37) — the audience was expected to smile not only at recognizing a reference to Ovid but also at the perception that the medieval poet has just given them a sly hint about Viola's character.

A further source of humor comes from Babio's futile attempts to play the lover and the gentleman (see Wailes). He is that favorite character of Roman comedy, the *senex amans*, the old man in love — a type whose amorous activities are doomed to failure. He aspires to the polite manners and generosity expected of the courtly hero, but his natural stinginess and poor education get in his way. He apes the discourse but bungles the grammar. Courtly romances are filled with lavish descriptions of elegant feasts and courteous behavior, both of which Babio desires to imitate. Thus when Croceus approaches, he orders the house to be made ready — by sweeping out the dung lying around! He makes a pretence of wanting to provide a feast for Lord Croceus but begrudges the expenditure of more than a farthing, and his idea of an elegant repast turns out to consist of half a chicken. Babio is not a gentleman *manqué* but an overt parody of the type. In yet another respect, the work appears to be a satire of *courtoisie*: it is misogynistic. The two women, Viola and Petula, are paragons of beauty and virtue only to the foolish Babio. In reality they are carnal schemers, out for their own pleasure and advantage (Brennan, p. 45).

ALDA
By William of Blois

Alda was written between 1167 and 1169 by William of
Blois, a Benedictine monk and brother of Peter of Blois, Arch-
deacon of Bath (for further information, see the introduction to
the edition of Marcel Wintzweiller, used for this translation).
In the prologue to the work, William declares that he is trans-
lating Menander, although nothing of Menander which has
survived corresponds with *Alda*. The few brief fragments of
Menander's *Androgynos* ("Man-Woman") are too brief to provide any reliable basis for comparison, and whatever the truth
about Menander's possible authorship of the work, it is impossible for anything like the "tail scene" to have come from the
decorous pen of the Greek playwright. Although I suspect the
attribution to Menander of being a polite fiction, it is barely
possible that William actually did base his tale upon a work of
Menander which was subsequently lost. When he composed
Alda, William was living in Sicily, having been appointed abbot
of the monastery of Santa Maria di Maniaco in the diocese of
Messina; Menander had not been entirely forgotten in the
East, for in the eleventh century Psellos was writing commentaries on him, and some of his plays, or more likely prose par-
aphrases of them, may have existed in Sicily in the twelfth
century (Wintzweiller, p. 115). In his prologue, William mentions an earlier, poor translation into Latin of the work by
Menander. On the other hand, it is at least as likely that William, perhaps having learned in Sicily something about Menander, ascribed the tale to him in an attempt to gloss over its
risqué nature and to give authority to an original creation, just
as a number of other medieval works — some, like *The Three
Girls* and the *Vetula,* quite frank about sexual matters — were
adorned with the dignity and *auctoritas* of Ovid's prestigious
name (see Spitzer, p. 415, for the importance of claiming a
written source).

At the outset William seems concerned to follow the conventions of Terentian drama, as he furnishes his plays with
both an argument and a prologue. Terence's *Eunuchus* in fact

also recounts the success of an opportunistic youth who, like Pyrrhus interested only in sex, gains access to an otherwise inaccessible girl by means of a clever disguise. The plot, known from classical times, is a variant of the Danaë archetype — the story of the beauteous maiden locked away from all masculine society by her stern father or aging husband and the enterprising lover who, often in disguise, successfully surmounts all obstacles and gets the girl. In the *Eunuchus* the ravished girl was actually gazing at a painting of Danaë when her suitor, inspired by that painting to imitate Jupiter, seized his opportunity.

In spite of the supposedly classical paternity of *Alda*, it soon becomes apparent that the work is thoroughly medieval. The Danaë theme was popular in the Middle Ages; Marie de France's "Lay of Guigemar" and the Provençal *Flamenca* are obvious examples. So, too, many of the characters will seem familiar to readers of medieval literature. The locked-up maiden, Alda, is described as the paragon of virtue and beauty familiar from Romance. Pyrrhus, pallid and weak with passion, is the typical lover suffering from "amour de loin" — "he loves the girl for her reputation and not for herself" (167). Another medieval favorite is present as well in the clever old woman who concocts the ruse by which Alda's father is deceived. But in spite of these characters common to much medieval literature, the tale is highly and amusingly original. It is, in fact, one of the first of its type. On reflection one discovers that the sense of familiarity arises from a knowledge of somewhat later vernacular literature. Edmond Faral wrote that "among the texts which we possess, it is the *Alda* which offers us the first finished example of the systematically realistic and deliberately dishonest tale" ("Le fabliau," 1924, p. 342).

Alda starts out in sentimentality and swiftly moves to cynicism. It opens with a long and pathetic scene (perhaps over-long for modern tastes) in which the grief-stricken husband laments the impending death of his wife. William may have felt it necessary, or perhaps just more interesting, to dramatize the traumatic circumstances which caused the

father to become so intensely involved with his daughter that
he locks her away from the world. But William's cynicism is
apparent in a later echo of the opening scene. The dying
mother comforts her husband by telling him that she will live
on in their child and will not therefore wholly perish; Pyrrhus
uses the identical argument in the seduction scene to persuade
the naive Alda to comply with his wishes.

William, indeed, reveals considerable enthusiasm for the
more cynical parts of his work. He devotes twelve stereotyped
lines to Alda's peerless beauty but describes the equally unri-
valed hideousness of Pyrrhus's deceitful servant, Spurius, in
twenty-two vividly imaginative lines (see Goldin, p. 29). The
marvelous *pâté en croute* which Spurius makes, then steals, is
depicted in loving detail, as are Spurius' equally disreputable
girl friend, Spurca, her wretched hovel, and the uncomfortable
night that Spurius spends there. William puts into Spurius'
mouth a long speech on the evil power of gifts, echoing many
themes common to moralistic writing (for example, the references to simony, 227-28), but Spurius is no disinterested mor-
alist; at the very first opportunity he steals for himself the gift
which he has just talked his master into sending to Alda. For
all her father's stern training, Alda, the seeming epitome of
virtue, throws herself into the joys of carnal love with an
abandon which matches, even surpasses, Pyrrhus' own. Nor is
the happy ending necessarily all that happy. Pyrrhus never
said a word about wanting to marry the girl. He is forced to
do so, not to save *her* reputation but that of his sister when she
is accused of being a hermaphrodite. If sensitivity concerning
one's sister's honor was as great in Sicily in William's day as
it has been in more recent times, the joke becomes even funnier — and blacker (I am indebted to Shedd's dissertation for
this point).

As one might expect, the combination of obscenity and
cynicism has shocked some critics, both medieval and modern,
even though there is evidence that *Alda* was considered suitable material for school reading in medieval times (Faral, "Le
fabliau," 1924, p. 342). In 1170 Peter of Blois wrote with
unconcealed relief that he had succeeded in calling back to the

ways of righteousness "that noble talent of my brother, master William, when it had degenerated into writing tragedies and comedies ... a servile occupation ... a pernicious vanity" (*PL* 207, col. 235). More recent critics as well have been shocked by the text's imaginative obscenity. In his bilingual edition of the work, Wintzweiller stated (in Cohen, I, p. 109, n. 2) that in his translation he "toned down the crudity of some terms," a course which the present translator has not followed, and Maurice Wilmotte declared of the "tail scene" that "the author of *Alda* put words into the mouth of a virgin and attributes a zest to her curiosity which few modern writers of pornography would dare to risk" (p. 177).

The text of *Alda* has been transmitted by six manuscripts of the thirteenth and fourteenth centuries, and a florilegium with quotations from the work exists in at least six copies (Wintzweiller, pp. 124-25). It appears to have enjoyed a modest popularity, as its influence can be seen in the thirteenth-century *Floris and Lirope* of Robert of Blois and in the fabliau *Trubert* (Faral, "Le Fabliau," 1924, p. 343). The work was copied by no less a scribe than Boccaccio (Bertini, 1977-78, p. 135), and Bertini argues for its influence on one of the bawdiest, and funniest, stories in the *Decameron*, the tale sometimes called in English "Putting the the Devil in Hell" (3.10).

LIDIA
By Arnulf of Orléans

Lidia has traditionally been ascribed to the rhetorician Matthew of Vendôme, but Faral ("Le fabliau," 1924) showed that it could not be his, and recent studies (Roy, Bertini) have made a strong case for Arnulf of Orléans as author. It was probably composed shortly after 1175 (Bertini, 1978, p. 208). Arnulf was a scholar, writer of commentaries on Ovid and Lucan, and very likely the author of another, less successful comedy, the *Miles Gloriosus*. *Lidia* is, however, the least Ovidian of the comedies (Lackenbacher, in Cohen, I, p. 217). It also enjoys the dubious honor, I think, of being the most cynical of all. The dark view of human nature in *Alda*, with its cast of selfish, greedy, and carnal characters, is somehow lightened by the ebullient humor and ingenuity. The characters of *Lidia* are more self-centered, even vicious, and the work lacks *Alda*'s wit.

Lidia is the most blatantly misogynistic of the Latin comedies. Other than her beauty, the heroine has not a single good quality to recommend her. Arnulf, moreover, sees her as typical of her sex. Love's madness is said to rage more violently in women than in men (37, 95 ff.). "Not a one," claims Lusca, "knows moderation, nor is modesty found in any" (105). Ten men would not be enough to satisfy a woman like Lidia (102). Such outspoken antifeminism, however, is not uncommon in the Middle Ages, especially in clerical circles (Schotter, pp. 19-33, and Brennan, p. 45).

Perhaps the most notable feature of Arnulf's comedy is its delight in rhetoric. Bruno Roy (p. 266) has characterized it as "the apotheosis of the pun." For example, the notion that ten men would not be enough to satisfy Lidia involves a pun on the name of Lidia's husband, Decius, and *decem*, the Latin word for "ten." Arnulf delights in punning upon Lidia's name and *ludus* or *ludere,* which can mean both "play," "sport" (with sexual connotations), and "deceive" (cf. "delusion"). Besides, the work is full of long descriptions, as in the elaborate description of Lidia (443-52), which includes a number of puns upon *ludus* and its derivatives. Such features, which a translation can do little to reproduce, were the height of fashion in the later twelfth century. They make it hard to avoid stiltedness in English.

The work survives in two fourteenth-century manuscripts, the second of which may have been copied by Boccaccio (Lackenbacher, p. 223). Whether or not Boccaccio was the actual scribe, he knew the tale and imitated it in *Decameron* 7.9, changing only the name of Decius to Nicostrato. Interestingly, the narrator for the seventh day is called Panfilo. The influence of the comedies on Boccaccio has been the subject of several brief studies and would repay further investigation

(Amorino, p. 335). Chaucer's "Merchant's Tale" reveals his debt to *Lidia*.

THE THREE GIRLS

The anonymous poem *The Three Girls (De Tribus Puellis)* probably dates to the twelfth or thirteenth century. Although the work is published in Cohen's and Bertini's collections of elegiac "comedies," it is narrative rather than dramatic. It shares with the comedies, however, an interest in Ovidian love and is written in elegiac couplets. It is preserved in two manuscripts of the fifteenth century and several incunables (Pittaluga in Bertini, 1976, pp. 281-88, and Reeve, pp. 131-33). In the manuscripts the work is ascribed to Ovid himself, but for all the Ovidianism of the subject and the very many quotations from and allusions to the *magister amoris*, the style and content suggest that it was written in the twelfth or thirteenth century, perhaps in France. According to Maury (in Cohen, II, p. 228), the poem is the work of a cleric who had read too much Ovid. It betrays the bookish learning and the naiveté of a scholar indulging in a not uncommon masculine fantasy: the girl does the wooing and does not play "hard to get."

In a version without the Latin text it is difficult to do full justice to the pervasive Ovidianism of this poem (full lists of Ovidian imitations can be found in the edition of Maury, and the discussions of Pittaluga [1976-77] and Hagendahl). The particularly playful, even naughty, use made of Ovid in *The Three Girls*, however, deserves special comment. Not only is the work an expansion of *Amores* 1.5, but it is at the same time a conscious perversion of it. In the Latin elegy, the poet is taking his afternoon siesta when Corinna, clad in the lightest of garments, bursts into his bedroom. Ovid impulsively rips off the transparent tunic, and Corinna puts up a sham struggle to retain her clothing, but "She fought like one not wanting to win, and so was her own betrayer" (15-16). When at last Corinna stands naked before the poet's delighted eyes, he gives us a discreet, four-line portrait of her naked charms, starting at the shoulders and ending with her hips and thighs. Ovid is never openly pornographic and knows when, and where, to stop. He clasps Corinna to him and the poem concludes with his contented prayer for many more such successful afternoons. The poem is a gem of erotic elegy, discreet and suggestive at once.

The medieval poet is a different sort. Unlike the impulsive Ovid, he feigns indifference, "pretending that I desired to return home" (163), thus making the girl entreat him to stay. Ovid had enjoyed his view of Corinna in the half-light of a shady bedroom (his poem devotes four lines to a description of the light); the medieval poet, once again striving, it seems, to out-Ovid Ovid, expatiates upon the golden firelight illuminating the body of his beloved (247 ff.). Ovid limited his description of Corinna to four lines; not so the medieval poet, who goes on for some ten lines before coyly concluding (261-63),

> I shall not tell you what next I saw,
> although I could describe far better sights if I wished —
> no, not a word . . .

The willing medieval maiden consciously exploits Ovid's remarks in the *Art of Love* (and perhaps those in *Pamphilus* as well) about the use of force (see the note to verse 281). The tip-off, however, to the playful use of Ovid occurs earlier, in the poet's request to enjoy the girl's virginity as his reward (Hagendahl, p. 253). Here he has borrowed and turned upside down Daphne's request to her father to remain perpetually a virgin *(Metamorphoses* 1.486-87):

> "da mihi perpetua, genitor carissime," dixit
> "virginitate frui"

> "Grant, dearest father," she said, "that I may enjoy perpetual virginity."

Compare the medieval request (142):

> "da michi, queso, tua virginitate frui."

"grant me, I beg, your virginity for my enjoyment."

The use or abuse is willful and funny. For an audience who knew Ovid by heart — the intended audience of this poem — the lesson was clear. Ovid was there to profit men and to give them pleasure, both literally and literarily.

The imprint of a medieval education is plain. In addition to the many quotations from classical authors, the taste for logical reasoning which a scholastic education inspired is evident. For example, in order to persuade her suitor to stay the night the heroine neatly enumerates, classifies, and analyzes three reasons: the night, love, and herself. The author reveals himself to be a good student of rhetoric as well. He knows all the devices recommended by the rhetorical handbooks and takes delight in their use. The poem, in fact, is little more than an *amplificatio* of *Amores* 1.5, adapted to a medieval setting (Maury, p. 229).

The highly rhetorical style makes this poem difficult to translate. Some of the balanced couplets, no doubt the author's pride and joy, sound artificial and flat in English. For example, 161-62:

Sed temptare volens—neque iam temptare nocebat—
Temptavi tandem calliditate mea.

And wishing to put her to the test (there was
no harm in trying), I devised this strategm . . .

The repetition of *temptare* ("attempt") three times in two lines might be considered artful in Latin; it sounds unimaginative in English. I have tried to retain the balance of the Latin where I could, but have not done so if the result sounded excessively silly.

EDITORIAL POLICY FOR THIS TRANSLATION

The remarks above about the translation of *The Three Girls* hold good in general for this volume. I have tried to remain faithful to the spirit of the Latin texts at all times, and to the letter when I could. The translations are not meant as "trots," and I have frequently been free in my renditions. Stage directions in square brackets are my additions; those without the brackets occur in the manuscripts. As noted above, the translation of *Pamphilus* is probably the most free, as it was intended for acting. The original texts were written in elegiac couplets. For my translations I have adopted what I consider to be closer to rhythmical prose than verse, and have generally used a four-stress line. I have tried to tread the middle ground between formality and colloquialism. These works are not truly colloquial but neither do they represent the high style, though parodies of the *stylus gravis* are frequent. In many ways, the works, replete with puns and grammatical jokes, resist translation. I have indicated at least some of the puns in the notes to the translations.

The choice of works to include was in some cases a difficult one. My decision was influenced by two factors: the overall quality of a particular work, coupled with its importance to the literary tradition. The selection of *Pamphilus* and *Geta* was easy, their inclusion justified by both their caliber and their popularity. *Alda* is simply one of the funniest works from the medieval (or any) period, while to my mind *The Three Girls* runs a close second. The *Aulularia* is perhaps duller than the rest, but it supplements the picture of parody of medieval scholasticism offered by *Geta*. The *Lidia*, for all its misogyny, claims our attention by its influence on both Boccaccio and Chaucer. Finally, it was with great regret that I omitted the *De Nuncio Sagaci*, but this work, the only one written in a meter other than the elegiac couplet, is fragmentary, and it raises too many questions for easy inclusion here. Perhaps I should have translated Matthew of Vendôme's *Milo*, but its rhetoric makes it particularly difficult to reproduce without the Latin text. For the others, I felt I simply had to stop somewhere.

I have not attempted a bilingual edition. For one person to make proper editions of works existing in sixty or more manuscripts, as is the case for *Pamphilus* or *Geta*, is impossible, nor, indeed, is there now a need for such work. Several of the plays have received fine modern critical editions, and Ferruccio Bertini and his colleagues at the University of Genoa are in the process of editing the entire corpus. For those who read Italian, these editions give both Latin and vernacular versions, and the older edition supervised by Gustave Cohen contains French translations.

I owe large debts of gratitude to many — above all, to my friends and former colleagues at the University of California, Santa Barbara, Donald Maddox, John R. Elliott, and Robert A. Potter, for encouraging me to continue my work on the comedies. My debt to Robert Potter and to his students who devoted many hours to the production of *Pamphilus* is enormous. I also must thank the editors of *Allegorica*, where two of the translations were first published, not only for permission to reprint but even more for the enthusiasm with which they greeted these versions, particularly *Alda*. James J. Wilhelm and Lowry Nelson, Jr., editors of the Garland Medieval Library, have been invariably helpful.

SELECT BIBLIOGRAPHY

I. EDITIONS AND TRANSLATIONS

Bate, A. Keith. *Three Latin Comedies*. Toronto Medieval Latin Texts, *6*. Pontifical Institute, 1976. Contains Latin texts of *Geta, Babio,* and *Pamphilus,* with brief introductions and notes.

Baudouin, Adolphe. *Pamphile, ou l'Art d'être aimé, comédie latine du Xe siècle.* Paris: Librairie Moderne, 1874. Incorporates the notes of the 1470 *editio princeps.*

Becker, Franz G. *Pamphilus. Prolegomena zum Pamphilus de amore und kritische Textausgabe.* Beihefte zum Mittellateinischen Jahrbuch, *9.* Ratingen/Düsseldorf, 1972.

Benson, Larry D., and Theodore M. Andersson. *The Literary Context of Chaucer's Fabliaux.* Indianapolis and New York: Bobbs-Merrill, 1971. Contains Lackenbacker's Latin text (from Cohen, I) and translation of *Lidia,* pp. 206-233, cited as a source of Chaucer's *Merchant's Tale.*

Bertini, Ferruccio. *La commedia elegiaca latina in Francia con un saggio di traduzione dell'Amphitryo di Vitale di Blois.* Genoa: Tilgher, 1973.

_____, ed. *Commedie latine del XII e XIII secolo.* 4 vols. Università di Genova: Istituto di Filologia Classica e Medievale. *1*: Sassari: Gallizzi, 1976. Critical editions with facing Italian translations of *Aulularia,* ed. Ferruccio Bertini; *De Afra et Milone,* ed. Paola Busdraghi; *Pamphilus, Gliscerium et Birria,* ed. Annamaria Savi; *De tribus puellis,* ed. Stefano Pittaluga.

_____, ed. *Commedie latine del XII e XIII secolo. 2,* 1980. Critical editions and Italian translations of *De nuntio sagaci*, ed. Gabriella Rossetti; *Babio*, ed. Andrea Dessà Fulgheri; *De tribus sociis*, ed. Enzo Cadoni; *De clericis et rustico*, ed. Enzo Cadoni.

_____, ed. *Commedie latine del XII e XIII secolo. 3*, 1980. Critical editions and Italian translations of *Pamphilus*, ed. Stefano Pittaluga; *Geta*, ed. Ferruccio Bertini; *Baucis et Traso*, ed. Giovanni Orlandi; *De Mercatore*, ed. Paola Busdraghi.

_____, ed. *Commedie latine del XII e XIII secolo. 4*, 1983. Critical editions and Italian translations of Arnulf of Orléans' *Miles gloriosus*, ed. Silvana Pareto; *De Lombardo et lumaca*, ed. Magda Bonacini; *Asinarius*, ed. Simona Rizzardi.

Brennan, Malcolm M. *Babio. A Twelfth Century Profane Comedy*. The Citadel Monograph Series, *7*. Charleston, S.C.: Military College of South Carolina, 1968.

Chevallier, Claude-Alain. *Théâtre comique du moyen-âge* Paris: 10/18, 1973. Contains a translation of *Babio*.

Cohen, Gustave, general ed. *La "Comédie" latine en France au XIIe siècle*. 2 vols. Paris: Société d'Edition "Les Belles-Lettres," 1931. Editions of fifteen works with facing French translations.

Crawford, James Martin. *The Secular Latin Comedies of Twelfth-Century France*. Dissertation, Indiana University, 1977. Introductions and English translations of Cohen's texts.

Elliott, Alison G. *"Alda." Allegorica, 1* (1976), 53-93. A translation, with facing Latin text (ed. Wintzweiller, in Cohen, I).

_____. *"Geta." Allegorica, 3* (1978), 9-61. A translation, with facing Latin text (ed. Guilhou, in Cohen, I).

Faral, Edmond. *De Babione.* Bibliothèque de l'Ecole des Hautes Etudes, *193.* Paris: Champion, 1948. Latin text with French translation; includes a long stylistic analysis, on the basis of which Faral dates the play in the second half of the 12th century, and a discussion of possible English origin.

Garbáty, Thomas Jay. *"Pamphilus, de Amore.* An Introduction and Translation." *Chaucer Review, 2* (1967), 109-34.

Rubio, L., and T. González Rolán. *Pánfilo, o El arte de amar.* Barcelona: Bosch, 1977. Bilingual edition which pays particular attention to the Spanish tradition.

II. OTHER PRIMARY TEXTS

Andreas Capellanus. *The Art of Courtly Love.* Trans. John Jay Parry. New York: Ungar, 1941; rpt. 1959.

Anstey, H., ed. *Monumenta Academica, or Documents Illustrative of Academical Life and Studies at Oxford.* Part 2, *Libri Cancellarii et Procuratorum.* Rolls Series, *50b.* London, 1868.

Elliott, Alison G. "The *Facetus* or, *The Art of Courtly Living.*" *Allegorica, 2* (1977), 27-57. Introduction and translation of a work directly influenced by *Pamphilus.*

Faral, Edmond. *Les Arts poétiques du XIIe et du XIIIe siècle.* Paris: Champion, 1924; rpt. 1958. The standard study and edition of the rhetorical treatises.

Giraldus Cambrensis. *Autobiography.* Ed. and trans. H. E. Butler. London: Jonathan Cape, 1937.

Huygens, R. B. C. *Accessus ad auctores, Bernard d'Utrecht, Conrad d'Hirsau.* Leiden: E. J. Brill, 1970. Contains the *accessus* to *Pamphilus*, p. 53.

Monaci, Ernesto. *Crestomazia italiana dei primi secoli.* Rome/
Naples: Società Dante Aligheri, 1955. Contains the version of *Pamphilus* in Venetian, pp. 182-86.

Morawski, Joseph de, ed. *Pamphile et Galatée par Jehan
Bras-de-Fer de Dammartin-en-Goële.* Paris: Champion,
1917. An Old French adaptation of *Pamphilus.*

Plautus. *Captivi,* ed. W. M. Lindsay. Methuen: London, 1900;
rpt. Arno Press: New York, 1979.

Ranstrand, Gunnar, ed. *Querolus sive Aulularia: Incerti auc-
toris comoedia una cum indice verborum.* Acta Universi-
tatis Gotoburgensis, *57* (1951:1). The source of Vitalis'
Aulularia.

Sextus Amarcius Gallus Piosistralus. *Sermonum Libri IV.* Ed.
M. Manitius. Leipzig: Teubner, 1888. Mentions a jongleur performing three of the *Cambridge Songs.*

III. CRITICAL STUDIES

Albin, Rochelle Semmel. "Psychological Studies of Rape."
Signs, 3 (1977), 423-35.

Amorino, Susanna Calliero. "L' *Alda* di Guglielmo di Blois ed
il *Ninfale Fiesolano* di Boccaccio." *Sandalion, 3* (1980),
335-43.

Axton, Richard. *European Drama of the Early Middle Ages.*
London: Hutchinson University Library, 1974. Discusses
the theatricality of *Babio.*

Bate, A. Keith. "Language for School and Court: Comedy in
Geta, Alda, and *Babio.*" *L'Eredità classica nel medioevo: il*

linguaggio comico. Atti del III Convegno di Studio. Viterbo: Agnesotti, 1978; pp. 3-33.

_____. "Twelfth-Century Latin Comedies and the Theatre." *ARCA, 3: Papers of the Liverpool Latin Seminar, 2* (1979); pp. 249-62. On the theatrical nature of the comedies. Bate addresses the question of audience.

Bertini, Ferruccio. "Il personaggio di Sardana nell'*Aulularia* di Vitale di Blois. Ipotesi sull'origine di un nome." *Medioevo Romanzo, 1* (1974), 365-74.

_____. "Una novella del Boccaccio e l'*Alda* di Guglielmo di Blois." *Maia, 29-30* (1977-78), 135-41.

_____. "La Commedia latina del XII secolo." In *L'Eredità classica nel medioevo: il linguaggio comico.* Atti del III Convegno di Studio. Viterbo: Agnesotti, 1979; pp. 63-80. A useful general survey.

_____. "Il *Geta* di Vitale di Blois e la scuola di Abelardo." *Sandalion, 2* (1979), 257-65. A discussion of the parody of Boethian logic.

Bianchi, Dante. "Per la commedia latina del sec. XII." *Aevum, 29* (1955), 171-78. Discussion of medieval definitions of comedy and their application to the Latin comedies.

Blumenthal, Wilfred. "Untersuchungen zur pseudo-ovidianischen Komödie *Pamphilus.*" *Mittellateinisches Jahrbuch, 11* (1976), 224-311. An exhaustive study of the play, with a long discussion of the work's debt to Ovid (pp. 224-46) and other classical authors, as well as an analysis of the use of rhetoric.

Brondsted. P. O. "The Medieval *Comedia*: Choice of Form." *Classica et Mediaevalia, 31* (1975), 258-68. Stresses the debt of the comedies to Roman elegy.

Curran, L. C. "Rape and Rape Victims in the *Metamorphoses.*"

Arethusa, 11 (1978), 213-41. Argues for Ovid's sympathetic understanding of rape victims.

Dronke, Peter. "The Rise of the Medieval Fabliau: Latin and Vernacular Evidence." *Romanische Forschungen, 85* (1973), 275-97. Seeks to show the ways Latin evidence can illuminate the vernacular; a brief discussion of the comedies on p. 282.

_____. "A Note on *Pamphilus.*" *Journal of the Warburg and Courtauld Institute, 42* (1979), 225-30. On the early date, possibly German origin, and theatricality. Dronke proposes only three characters.

Elliott, Alison G. "The Bedraggled Cupid: Ovidian Satire in *Carmina Burana* 105." *Traditio, 37* (1981), 426-37. The medieval poet "understood" Ovid's ironic stance.

_____. "The Art of the Inept *Exemplum*: Ovidian Deception in *Carmina Burana* 117 and 178." *Sandalion, 5* (1982), 27-42. On the ironic use of an untrustworthy narrator.

Faral, Edmond. *Les Jongleurs en France au moyen âge.* Bibliothèque de l'Ecole des Hautes Etudes, *187.* Paris: Champion, 1910; rpt. 1964. Comprehensive survey of the activities of jongleurs.

_____. "Le fabliau latin au moyen âge." *Romania, 50* (1924), 321-85. A major study of genre. Faral considers that the text originated from the rhetorical preoccupations of the French cathedral schools and suggests that the Latin works were the models for the vernacular fabliaux.

Friedman, Lionel J. "Gradus Amoris." *Romance Philology, 19* (1965), 167-77.

Frye, Northrop. *The Anatomy of Criticism.* Princeton: University Press, 1957; rpt. 1973.

Gaiser, Konrad. *Menanders "Hydria." Eine hellenistiche Komödie und ihr Weg ins lateinische Mittelalter.* Heidelberg, 1977. In a long concluding chapter Gaiser tries to trace the steps by which Hellenistic Greek comedy could have exerted an influence on the medieval works.

Garbáty, Thomas Jay. "The *Pamphilus* Tradition in Ruiz and Chaucer." *Philological Quarterly, 46* (1967), 457-70. Besides noting the citations of *Pamphilus* in "The Tale of Melibee" and "The Franklin's Tale," Garbáty lists extensive parallels with the *Troilus* (pp. 495 ff.).

Gilson, Etienne. *The History of Christian Philosophy in the Middle Ages.* New York: Random House, 1955.

Goldin, Daniela. "Lettura dell'*Alda* di Guglielmo di Blois." *Cultura Neolatina, 40* (1980), 17-32. A close reading of the text with particular attention to rhetoric.

Gougenheim, Georges. "Le mime Vitalis." *Mélanges d'histoire du théâtre du Moyen âge et du Renaissance, offerts à Gustave Cohen.* Paris: Niset, 1950; pp. 29-33.

Gybbon-Monypenny, G. B. *"Dixe la por te dar ensiempro*: Juan Ruiz's Adaptation of the *Pamphilus.*" In Gybbon-Monypenny, ed., *"Libro de Buen Amor" Studies.* London: Tamesis, 1970; pp. 123-48.

Hagendahl, Harald. "La 'Comédie' latine au XIIe siècle et ses modèles antiques." In ΔΡΑΓΜΑ, *Martino P. Nilsson dedicatum.* Acta Instituti Romani Regni Sueviae. Lund, 1939; pp. 222-55. A source-study, with many specific examples, particularly of imitations of Ovid.

Haller, Robert S. "The *Altercatio Phyllidis et Florae* as an Ovidian Satire." *Mediaeval Studies, 30* (1968), 119-33. The poem is ironic, seeming to praise what it blames.

Haskins, Charles Homer. *The Renaissance of the Twelfth Century.* Cambridge: Harvard University Press, 1927; rpt.

1976.

Henshaw, Millett. "The Attitude of the Church to the Stage to the End of the Middle Ages." *Medievalia et Humanistica, 7* (1952), 3-17. A comprehensive survey of attitudes.

Hunningher, Benjamin. *The Origin of the Theater.* Westport, Ct.: Greenwood Press, 1955; rpt. 1978.

Hunt, Tony. "Chrestien and the *Comediae.*" *Mediaeval Studies, 40* (1978), 120-56. Shows the influence of the comedies on Chrétien, particularly in *Cligès* and the *Chevalier au lion.*

_____. "Aristotle, Dialectic, and Courtly Literature." *Viator, 10* (1979), 95-129. Pages 123-25 discuss the parody of dialectic in *Geta.*

_____. "'Prodesse et Delectare': Metaphors of Pleasure and Instruction in Old French." *Neuphilologische Mitteilungen, 80* (1979), 17-35.

Jones, L. W., and C. R. Morey. *The Miniatures of the MSS of Terence Prior to the Thirteenth Century.* 2 vols. Princeton: University Press, 1931.

Lacy, Gregg F. "Fabliau Stylistic Humor." *Kentucky Romance Quarterly, 26* (1979), 349-57. Confined to Old French texts but with important implications for the Latin works, especially on the parody of the *gravis stilus.*

Lecoy, Félix. *Recherches sur le "Libro de buen amor."* Paris: Droz, 1938. Lecoy gives tables of correspondences between *Pamphilus* and the *Libro de buen amor* (pp. 309-17).

Lehmann, Paul. *Die Parodie im Mittelalter.* Stuttgart: Anton Heisermann, 1963. The standard study of medieval Latin parody.

Lida de Malkiel, María Rosa. "Una interpretación más de Juan Ruiz." *Romance Philology, 14* (1961), 228-37. An important review article, with much discussion of the influence of *Pamphilus* on the *Libro de buen amor.*

Marshall, Mary Hatch. "'Theatre' in the Middle Ages: Evidence from the Dictionaries and Glosses." *Symposium, 4* (1950), 1-39, 366-89.

_____. "Boethius' Definition of *Persona* and Mediaeval Understanding of the Roman Theater." *Speculum, 25* (1950), 471-82. Argues that in the twelfth century scholars had some knowledge of the representation of formal drama in the ancient world.

Neumann, Günter. "Menanders *Androgynos*." *Hermes, 81* (1953), 491-96. Menander was only an indirect source for William of Blois, who was more directly influenced by Vitalis of Blois; the motif of seduction facilitated by an exchange of clothing does ultimately go back first to Euripides and then to Menander.

Nicoll, Allardyce. *Masks, Mimes, and Miracles: Studies in the Popular Theatre.* New York: Harcourt Brace, 1931.

Noonan, John T., Jr. "Power to Choose." *Viator, 4* (1973), 419-34. On changing attitudes toward marriage and the importance of the doctrine of consent in the twelfth century.

Nykrog, Per. *Les Fabliaux.* Publications Romanes et Françaises, *123.* Geneva: Droz, 1973.

Ogilvy, J. D. A. "Mimi, Scurrae, Histriones: Entertainers of the Early Middle Ages." *Speculum, 38* (1963), 603-19. Argues for theater in the early Middle Ages.

Pearcy, Roy J. "Investigations into the Principles of Fabliau Structure." In *Versions of Medieval Comedy,* ed. Paul G. Ruggiers. Norman: University of Oklahoma, 1977; pp.

67-100. Explores the proposition that the fabliaux are concerned with epistemology.

Pirot, F. *Recherches sur les connaissances littéraires des troubadours occitans et catalans des XIIe et XIIIe siècles.* Memorias de la Real Academia de Buenas Letras, *14*. Barcelona, 1972.

Pittaluga, Stefano. "Le *De tribus puellis*, 'comédie Ovidenne.'" *Vita Latina*, *61* (1976), 2-13, and *62* (1977), 2-14. Argues that *The Three Girls* is easily the most "Ovidian" of the comedies.

_____. "Alano di Lilla e la *rimula Veneris.*" *Maia*, *31* (1979), 147-50.

_____. "Echi Terenziani nel *Pamphilus.*" *Studi Medievali*, *23* (1982), 297-302. Posits a direct knowledge of *Pamphilus*, not merely one drawn from florilegia.

Reeve, Michael D. "Early Editions of *De tribus puellis.*" *Mittellateinisches Jahrbuch*, *15* (1980), 131-33. Additions and corrections to Pittaluga's edition.

Rico, Francisco. "Sobre el origen de la autobiografía en el *Libro de buen amor.*" *Anuario de Estudios Medievales*, *4* (1967), 301-25. On the importance of the fact that *Pamphilus* was considered an autobiography.

Roy, Bruno. "Arnulf of Orléans and the Latin 'Comedy.'" *Speculum*, *49* (1974), 258-66. Publishes an important gloss of Arnulf showing that he thought that *Pamphilus* was a stage-play. On Arnulf's own contribution to the theater.

Schmidt, Wieland. *Untersuchungen zum "Geta" des Vitalis Blesensis.* Suppl. to *Mittellateinisches Jahrbuch*, *14*. Ratingen-Düsseldorf, 1975.

Schotter, Anne Howland. "Women's Song in Medieval Latin."

In *Vox Feminae: Studies in Medieval Women's Song*. Ed. John F. Plummer. Studies in Medieval Culture, *15*. Kalamazoo: Western Michigan University, 1981; pp. 19-33. Medieval Latin women's song, as poetry whose audience as well as whose authors were male, presents a distinctly masculine view of woman's experience in love (p. 30).

Seidenspinner de Núñez, Dayle. "The Poet as Badger: Notes on Juan Ruiz's Adaptation of the *Pamphilus*." *Romance Philology, 30* (1976), 123-34. Discusses the parodic and didactic intention of Ruiz's adaptation.

Shedd, Gordon M. *Amor Dethroned: The Ovidian Tradition in Courtly Love Poetry*. Dissertation, Pennsylvania State University, 1965. Argues for an ironic reading of many texts, including several comedies.

Spitzer, Leo. "Note on the Poetic and the Empirical 'I' in Medieval Authors." *Traditio, 4* (1946), 414-22.

Sticca, Sandro. *The Latin Passion Play: Its Origins and Development*. Albany: State University of New York Press, 1970.

Suchomski, Joachim. *"Delectatio" und "Utilitas"*. *Ein Beitrag zum Verständnis mittelalterlicher komischer Literatur*. Bern/Munich: Franke, 1975. The individual comedies are discussed on pp. 110-42.

Thompson, Ian. "Latin 'Elegiac Comedy' of the Twelfth Century." In *Versions of Medieval Comedy*, ed. Paul G. Ruggiers. Norman: University of Oklahoma, 1977; pp. 51-66. The purpose of Thompson's study is to discuss briefly questions of genre and to provide a general description of the works and notes on the comic force of the poems (p. 52).

Ugolini, Marco. "Fondamenti per una analisi testuale dell' *Alda* di Guglielmo di Blois." *Sandalion, 3* (1980), 323-34.

Largely a study of possible sources.

Vinay, Gustavo. "La commedia latina del secolo XII." *Studi medievali, 18* (1952), 209-71. A perceptive and important discussion of genre.

Waddell, Helen. *The Wandering Scholars*. London: Constable, 1945. A lively description of the activities of the so-called Goliards.

Wailes, Stephen L. "Role-Playing in Medieval *Comediae* and Fabliaux." *Neuphilologische Mitteilungen, 75* (1974), 640-49. The humor derives from the actors' playing of roles unsuited to them, specifically the enacting by socially inferior persons of parts appropriate to the higher classes (p. 640).

Webber, Edwin J. "The *Celestina* as an *Arte de Amores.*" *Modern Philology, 45* (1958), 145-53. Includes a discussion of the influence of *Pamphilus*.

PAMPHILUS[1]

[enter Pamphilus, alone]

PAMPHILUS: I'm wounded. Here, deep in my heart
lies buried a secret injury.
My wound grows continually worse,
but as yet I do not even dare to speak aloud
the name of what has struck me down.
The wound itself must be unnamed, hidden from all eyes.
Thus my future is bleak; no medicine can cure me.   5
How can I find a better course to follow?
Alas, what am I to do? I'm so very unsure.
I complain, and my complaints are justified
for there is nowhere I can turn for advice.   10
But since there is much that harms me,
I need to seek much help.
If I were to name the true nature of my wound,
from where it comes, and who has dealt the blow,
I would likely destroy all hope of ever being cured.   15
Hope can revive a man; it can destroy him too.
But if on the contrary I conceal forever
the nature and cause of my pain, seeking no cure,
perhaps even worse will befall me,
and I shall die for love.   20
I think that revealing is better.
The fire that is hidden burns the more fiercely;
spread about, it glows, then dwindles to ashes.
Therefore I will speak to Venus,
for Venus is death or life to me;
her advice will guide the future course
of all my affairs.

[to Venus]

Only hope of my life, illustrious Venus, hail!   25
Thou who makest all things subservient to thy will,
thou whom lofty princes fear,
to whom all-potent kings are servant,

1

Pamphilus

thou, o holy one, mercifully
consider a humble petitioner's prayers.
    Don't be hard on me; don't resist my prayers;
just do what I ask. I'm not asking anything very great —   30
"not very great," yet it seems so to me in my misery.
Nevertheless, it wouldn't be difficult for you to grant.
Just say "yes," and then, oh then, I shall be truly blessed;
all things will go well for me.
    I have (how I wish that I didn't,   35
if your grace doesn't come to my aid),
I have a neighbor, a girl.
A fire nearby does more damage than one at a distance;
if she lived further away, she'd pain me less.
They say she's as beautiful as any woman of the town;
either love has deceived me or she surpasses them all.   40
She has sorely pierced my heart,
and I'm too weak to remove her from my thoughts.
My anguish increases with each passing hour;
I look worse and worse; I grow weak;
my healthy complexion pales.
I have spoken of this to no one,²
not even spoken the name of her who has wounded me,   45
and the reason which forbade me to speak was a good one.
It would be said (and I admit it)
that she is more nobly born than I;
therefore I fear to reveal my desire.
It would be said (and it is true)
that her family is richer than mine.
Riches and beauty always want the same for themselves,   50
and I have neither gifts to give
nor shining honor nor great wealth.
All that I have, I get by my hard work.
If she's rich, a girl can be
a plowman's daughter and still choose
whatever man she wishes from a thousand.
A trembling seizes my body at the sight of her beauty,   55
further preventing me from speaking of my desire.
Confident in her beauty, such a woman grows vain
and loses all sense of moderation.
I have tried to tear these cares from my heart,

2

but love burns more fiercely the more one resists it. 60
  There, you see my plight; there, you know my danger.
Be merciful, I pray, and grant my prayers.
  You're not answering me; you lend no ear to my words;
your clear eyes show me no light.
Either take your arrows out of my heart 65
or give me my desire! Who can endure
your arrows in his heart, your cruel fires,
such great labors of love, without a reward for his tears?
Even as I tender my just prayers, anxiety overwhelms me
and inspires my unceasing supplication. 70

Then Venus said:
    "Bold and persistent labor conquers all."[3]
So even you can enjoy the fruit of your labor.
Moreover, fear not to reveal your heart to anyone;
scarcely one woman in a thousand will turn you down.
Though at first she may sternly reject your entreaties, 75
her harsh words have little substance.
The boldly persistent buyer obtains the things
the seller at first swore were not for sale;
nor would the sailor have crossed the sea
had he been afraid when first the turbulent waves 80
battered his ship. Therefore, if at first
she does not look upon your request with favor,
art and good offices will make her compliant.
Art breaks down resistance and overthrows mighty cities;
by art castles fall; by art heavy burdens are made light;
by art fish are caught beneath the clear waters; 85
by art a man can cross the sea with dry feet.
In many things art gives aid — and good offices too.
The poor man owes his dinner to good offices;
good offices assuage the prince's anger, just though it may be,
and preserve the guilty unharmed in body or fortune. 90
It is, moreover, thanks to good offices
that the rich man laughs, who wept when he was poor,
that he now rides who once was forced to walk.
Those worldly goods which parents could not give,
good offices will grant to its ardent devotee.
If, then, at first your good offices she refuses, 95

3

you must stand prepared to be her humble servant.
Thus will you overcome her protests, which are but pretexts;
she will become your friend, who once was your enemy.
    Frequent those places where she can be found.
If you're good at telling pretty jokes, tell them;   100
young people always love fun and foolish tales,
and such things move the young to love.
And always show her a smiling face;
everyone looks more handsome when happy.
Neither be too silent, nor yet too talkative;   105
mere trifles often turn a girl against a man.
A sweet wit arouses and nourishes love
and softens the hardest heart.
    If you get the chance, woo her with gentle violence.[4]
What you scarcely hoped for soon she will offer herself.   110
Modesty now and then may keep her from admitting desire;
what she most desires to have she denies most strongly,
thinking it better to lose her virginity by force
than to say, "Do with me what you will."
    Be especially careful, if your worldly resources are small,   115
that she remain ignorant of your poverty;
with very little expense, ingenuity contrives
a pleasing appearance, conceals tears with a cheerful smile.
You can pretend to be what you're not in both words and dress;
a great success may depend on a little ingenuity.   120
Many things there are in the world which even your neighbor
does not know. Out of this contrive useful tales to tell her.
Believe me, often people get what they want by lying,
and telling the whole truth at times does harm.
    Those servants, male and female, who talk frequently   125
with her, be sure to win them over
to your cause with words and gifts
so they in turn will speak well of you
and fill their mistress's ears with your praises.
And if doubtfully she hesitates, the ignorant girl,
wondering whether she should do what you want,   130
that's the moment to wear down her resistance with temptations
so that swiftly, victoriously, you can enjoy your love.
A mind in doubt is swayed by a little hard labor.
    Moreover, it is a good idea for you both

4

to have a go-between who can discreetly bear your messages,   135
for envious old age discerns the doings of youth,
and, delighting to make trouble, prevents them from speaking.
        Begin! Time has given you already,
and will give you, better than you expect.
No need to fear those things that you fear now.   140
I shall not say another word to you;
work hard and you will win the girl.
There will be a thousand ways to finish
the work that you've begun.

PAMPHILUS: The healthy man freely offers consolation,
but the sick man doesn't feel any less ill.
My pain is not assuaged by Venus' words.   145
Love still rages in my sad heart.
Up to now, all my hope lay in Venus;
my hope has fled; my sorrow remains.
Poor shipwrecked wretch that I am, the pilot has left me adrift,
and I cannot find the fair harbor I seek.   150
What am I to do now? I can think only of Galathea.
I must go try to speak to her once again.

[Galathea enters]

How beautiful! God! She comes with her hair uncovered.
What an opportunity to speak to her now!
But all of a sudden I'm so overcome by emotion   155
I've lost my senses. The words won't come,
I feel weak, my hands and feet are trembling.
I'm so upset; this is no way for me to impress her.
In my mind I'd prepared so many things to say to her,
but fear has driven out everything I meant to say.   160
I am not the man I was; I scarcely recognize myself.
My voice won't come out right, but I'll speak to her anyway.

[to Galathea]

    My cousin from the next town sends you a thousand greetings
through me, commending her good offices to you.
She knows you by name and reputation only,   165

5

but desires, if opportunity arises, to make your acquaintance.
That town is filled with my relatives,
very distinguished people, who wanted to keep me there;
they were betrothing me to a girl with a very large dowry
and many other advantages not worth mentioning now.   170
I've put them all off.
You are the only girl who pleases me;
for you I'd give up everything in the world.

GALATHEA: You're joking, of course;[5]
young men often talk this way, but no one
quarrels over little stories made up for fun.

PAMPHILUS: Come now, let's tell each other our hearts' secrets,   175
and let no other soul know what's passed between us.
Let's promise, thus.[6] Then I'll speak,
and we must agree to tell the truth.
I am the first to begin; I'll speak the first.
No one in the world pleases me more than you.   180
Since I fell in love with you, three years have passed,
but I never dared tell you of my desire.
To the deaf the wise do not speak long.
I did not wish to speak in vain.
I love you steadfastly, but I will say no more   185
until you let me know your pleasure.

GALATHEA: Thus many a man has tempted many a maid,
and guileful love has deceived so many girls.
You planned to turn my head by speech or by art,
and it was wrong of you to deceive me with such guile.   190
Go seek other girls more suited to your filthy ways
whom you can beguile with false promises, with tricks.

PAMPHILUS: How often are the sins of the wicked
visited upon the innocent! I am condemned
for others' misdeeds, not for my own.
But please be gracious enough to listen to me   195
and let me say a few words to the mistress of my heart.
May God in heaven and the saints on earth be my witnesses,
I am not saying these things to deceive or beguile.

There is in this world no girl more lovely than you;
I've seen no one more dear. But I speak in vain.   200
Your youthful heart cannot distinguish
between those with evil intentions and those with good,
although the young are more perceptive than the old —
for the old see many things, but the young see more.
You are young; you must get to know me,   205
who I am, what my condition is, and what my love.
In these matters discretion is learned by experience;
experience and art teach us all we know.
To come and go, to talk, to converse with you,
to be together, that's *all* I ask.   210
Without conversation, we will never know the heart's depths.
Tell me, now, does all this please you?

GALATHEA: To come and go, to talk, that I don't forbid to you,
or to anyone. The streets belong rightly to all.
It is proper, and courteous too,   215
that a young girl reply to those who address her,
and greet by name those whom she sees;
this I grant freely enough to you,
or to anyone who comes by. When you come,
I'll greet you always in accord with my honor.
It is all right for a girl to listen and reply;
these actions are quite suitable in moderation.   220
And if you joke with me, I'll joke in reply,
just so long as the joking remains innocent.
You ask that we "be together"; I refuse to be alone with you.
It isn't seemly to be alone with a man;
being alone is dangerous; it gives birth to scandal.   225
I'll speak to you somewhat more safely in public.

PAMPHILUS: You have just given me not a small but a great reward.
To talk with you, that's entirely enough for me.
I can never thank you as richly as you deserve;
this kindness is too great for words to express.   230
        But perhaps there will come a time, a day,
when one could demonstrate that he's your real friend.
Lest I displease you, I don't dare say anything more,
though I would like to ask just one little favor —

7

that we should, if we get the chance,
exchange kisses, embraces, caresses....   235

GALATHEA: Although embraces nourish illicit love,
and caresses often betray a girl,
one favor I will allow, if you go no further,
and I won't allow these liberties to anyone but you.   240
         [she lets him kiss her hand]
But right now my parents are coming back from the temple
and I must go home, lest I be scolded.
There will be time enough for us to talk together;
let each of us remember what has passed between us.

        [exit Galathea]

PAMPHILUS: There is not, there never has been,   245
anyone happier than I in the whole world.
My anchor has caught fast on the desired shore.
God and Fortune have made me ecstatic with joy;
I return rich, who was poor when I left.
No need for her to ask me to remember her;
not even grief itself could drive her from my thoughts.   250
But her feelings aren't as strong as mine;
she doesn't know how much I desire her.
My feelings haven't changed at all;
just let her think about me, as I do about her.
    I've settled many problems, but still more
remain; oh, I don't know what I am to do.
If I am her attentive suitor,
always talking and joking with her,   255
gossiping rumor will fill the streets with talk of us.
But if I don't firm up this friendship by seeing her often,
perhaps our love, as yet infirm, will fade away.
With familiarity, love increases; it may diminish without it.
Unnourished love grows weak,   260
but fires increase with continual fueling —
take the fuel from the hearth, straightway the flame goes out.
    I am beset by great cares and great dangers;
I am tormented by indecision.
I see no hope for success in this affair;   265

8

my mind perceives no safe course of action.
Sometimes Fortune opposes men's actions,
preventing their plans from bearing fruit.
Thus many Fortune harms, but many it also blesses;
everyone in this world lives at its mercy.   270
God and hard work give us everything in this world,
but work can accomplish nothing without God.
Therefore may God be my guardian, the guide of my work;
may He govern all my work and my plans.
    As go-between I'll have neither brother nor cousin;   275
one would be rash to look for good faith there;
cousin does not keep faith with cousin, nor brother
with brother, when love's madness seizes them.
Little things do harm which the wise man can avoid;
therefore I must travel a different road.   280
Nearby lives an old woman, subtle, crafty,
a useful handmaiden of the arts of Venus.
I shall put my worries behind me
and go and tell her of my plan.

[*to the Bawd*]

    Having heard of your praises, of your reputation   285
for virtue, I have come to you for advice.
Please be good enough, gracious enough, to hear me,
but you mustn't tell another soul of this without my consent.
    I'm in love with my neighbor — you know her well —
Galathea, and she by her own words,   290
unless I'm mistaken, loves me too.
But I can't speak with her as I would like
for I must avoid a thousand dangers,
and I'm so concerned that everything frightens me.
Rumors — the smallest thing gives birth to them,   295
and once born, they're slow to die;
even rumors based on lies expand as they circulate.
You see our problem; let your voice go between us;
and I beg you, conceal our offenses as you go.

BAWD: Another man loves what you love;
what you seek, that another seeks also —

9

but as yet he does not have my assistance.   300
He is a proper man, worthy of a noble wife,
but I didn't like what he promised as my reward.
He promised me a fur-lined cloak and some other old clothes;
such cheap gifts have cost him my aid.
Given at the appropriate moment,   305
a gift confers great advantage.
Justice and the law give way before the power of gifts.
In my opinion, no one can have the girl you seek
without my aid; she is completely in my power.
I am her guide, her confidante; she listens to me in everything.   310
But I mustn't stand here talking to you for long;
I've other business to attend to.
"Heaven helps those who help themselves."

PAMPHILUS: This affair outweighs everything else with me,
and I've no other business to attend to.
Give me Galathea: you'll have given me everything.
                              [*aside*]
It is often necessary to procure the services of others;   315
                              [*to the Bawd*]
your services will receive their just reward.
If you'll look after my affairs, believe me,
in no way will I slight your labor
which I need so desperately. Just name your price;
I will give you whatever you ask.   320

BAWD: They want much, need much, those whom poverty oppresses;
I am ashamed to tell you how poor I am.
I had great wealth when my youth was in flower;
now my goods have slipped away; I am so very poor.
Feebleness has wholly destroyed me, and old age too;   325
all my art and my labor bring me no profit.
If you would enjoy the benefit of my assistance,
I request you to open your house to me.

PAMPHILUS: My house and everything are at your disposal;
I put all of my wealth at your command.   330
I am delighted with this agreement between us —
may keeping true faith be our mutual concern.

I pray you, then, make ready your cleverness and labors,
and take care of this matter in your own way.
Keep a prudent eye out from beginning to end,   335
for all praise and blame depends on the outcome.
Consider how you'll begin, consider your end;
with forethought you'll speak more persuasively.

[*exit Pamphilus; enter Galathea*]

BAWD [*pretending not to see Galathea*]:
    There lives in this town the most handsome young man,
and his good moral character increases in every way.   340
There has not been in our times a better or a sweeter man;
he has most generously undertaken to aid me in my poverty.
He excels all his peers in every virtue —
Pamphilus outstrips all his comrades in reputation.
With fools he is foolish, ' with the meek as gentle as a lamb.   345
It is the wise man who is in control of his own folly.
No, in worth he has no rival in the city.
Gluttony does not devour the goods he's acquired.
He is indeed honorable, for he comes of a fine family:
good fruit grows only on good trees.   350
Nature thus puts her seal of blessing on the offspring,
so often is the son like the father....
    But look, is that Galathea I see standing at the door?
Can she have heard what I was saying?
    I didn't think anyone was here just now, Galathea;   355
still, I spoke nothing but the truth.
Pamphilus certainly outshines all the men in this city;
it's remarkable how well he orders his life.
In him, all honor, laud and glory are ever increasing, [8]
and rightly no one begrudges him that.   360
He has great wealth but it has not made him proud,
nor is there anything criminal in his riches.
He's the man I would like for your husband, Galathea,
and you would want him too if you were wise.
    There, I've told you what I think
(though, of course, he never asked me to);   365
it was my own idea to join you two,
and your beauty and virtue and birth agree with me

11

that you two deserve to have each other.
These are but idle words to while away the time,
yet from little things do great things blossom,   370
and from a tiny spark great fires are born.
My mind has conceived the very beginning of this idea,
and I have undertaken to speak of it, as is my nature.
    But tell me, do these ideas move your mind and heart?   375
Are they pleasing or displeasing, I beg you, tell me?
I won't reveal to anyone what you've said
if you want it to remain concealed;
if you want it to be conveyed, I'll do so.
Tell me, don't hesitate. Put aside foolish modesty.
Silly girl, this modesty shows your inexperience.   380

GALATHEA: I am not a child!
It is not foolish modesty that prevents me from speaking;
I simply wonder what inspired your speech.
Yes, I wonder was it chance, or Pamphilus, that sent you to me?
Do you speak in expectation of some reward?

BAWD: As always, the crimes of the wicked impede the actions   385
of the just. How often are they punished undeservedly!
Although I am poor, I look for no rewards.
I am satisfied with my poverty.
And as I've told you, these were my own ideas;
no one else knows; there's no conspiracy.   390
It's merely this — if you two wish to meet together,
you can both do so without shame.
He is indeed noble, and you are no less
(I know both of your genealogies by heart).
He is more handsome than his comrades,   395
you are more beautiful than yours. It is right
and proper that beauty associate with beauty.
Equal wealth and equal age, these give their approval;
even public opinion would approve, if ever it should know.
You lack nothing but love alone.   400

GALATHEA: The things you are telling me
you ought to be telling my family and friends.
I desire only the husband of whom they approve.

Speak to them first, either you or that Pamphilus.
The affair will prosper if it pleases them.

BAWD: Of course your parents must approve of your marriage,   405
but meanwhile let your passion do battle with his.
Venus the clever keeps busy the hearts of the young,
who grow in guile through study of her ways.
She inflames hearts, gives to the generous, hates the stingy.
She pursues joy, flees sorrow. No one can put into words   410
the inestimable enjoyments of Venus.
Unless you obey her, you will never know.

GALATHEA: Through the rites of Venus, a virgin can lose her honor.
Love's fiery madness knows no restraint.
The shafts of Cupid inflict grievous wounds,   415
vilely seducing the unwary girl.
And thus gossip accuses even the innocent,
for biting envy never ceases its attack.
I should agree to what you seek if I did not fear gossip,
which brings to light even the most secret affairs of the heart.   420

BAWD: In these matters, infamy always seems greater than truth,
but truth, in the end, does triumph;
rumor is wholly defeated.
Whispers, rumors, worries, I shall remove all fear of them;
I shall discreetly conceal you and your sport.
I know all the rites of Venus and her ways.   425
You will be safe, thanks to my skill.

GALATHEA: When I see him, tell me what to say;
I'll speak the more safely
if you tell me first what to say.
I hesitate to mention my secret desire;
Deceit everywhere sets its snares.   430
But I shall put your good faith and your tongue to the test
and see where your cleverness leads me.
      Pamphilus himself has already asked for my love,
and the bonds of true friendship have joined us together.
But conceal this carefully, I beg you; tell only him.   435
But don't begin by speaking in this fashion.

13

First, make trials of his feelings; perhaps he himself
will tell you the sort of thing I've said.
Go now, and I beg, do everything discreetly.
Come tomorrow and tell me all he said to you.   440

BAWD [*to Pamphilus*]: How often are men disappointed in their hope
and all their labor. Pamphilus, things are not going well.
You have called me too late to your assistance.
Now neither my art nor my good offices can help you.
It is clear — they're preparing to marry off Galatea.   445
I am amazed at the decorations about her house.
There are a hundred reasons why I suspect this,
but her parents are keeping it carefully concealed.
Accept what I'm telling you
more like a reasonable man, I beg you.
Forget that which cannot be; seek only that which can.   450

PAMPHILUS: Woe is me!
Where has my strength and the use of my limbs gone?
My mind fails me, my tongue no longer serves me.
Alas, poor me!
My limbs are powerless; they deny me their service.
My hope has destroyed me,   455
the hope that Venus nourished in my bones.
Now hope has abandoned me, love's fire remains.
My ship nowhere can see its harbor;
my anchor can touch no bottom. In my affliction
I don't know where to turn for salvation;
Galathea alone offered me deliverance.   460
If I can't have her, then let me die!

BAWD: Fool, are you mad? Why this useless grief?
Your moaning and groaning will not gain you a thing.
Let restraint and prudence temper your weeping.   465
Dry your tears. Consider what you must do.
Great need engenders great courage,
and very often it makes a man clever.
With industrious skill, a man can conquer great dangers;
labor and vigilant art will find a solution.   470

PAMPHILUS: Alas, what labor can overcome such calamity?
All my hopes have perished; the hour of her wedding is at hand.
She can't marry while her husband lives,
and adultery is a crime.
All my labor has come to naught.   475
My worries are past cure;
by day, by night, no repose, no comfort,
only unrequited love gnawing at my woeful heart.

BAWD: How often does great grief vanish in a brief instant.
Gentle rains calm the great gale;   480
a tranquil day is the more welcome after long storms;
and after illness, health is the more welcome.
Now, cheer up! Grief, weeping, anger, away with them all!
Great joys are about to dispel your sorrow;
your Galathea will do what we wish;   485
she will put herself entirely in my hands.

PAMPHILUS: Just as with empty promises a doting mother
comforts her weeping children, so you perhaps
feed me on false hopes to ease my heart's pain.   490

BAWD: Even when it has escaped the hawk's cruel talons,
the sparrow hesitates, thinking that danger lurks everywhere.
There is no reason for me to lie to you.
You will find that everything I have said is true!

PAMPHILUS: If you are telling me the truth   495
(and if she was telling you the truth),
then every true cause for sorrow has fled my heart.
But a good beginning does not ensure a good end;
accidents often spoil the tasks we've begun.

BAWD: No man can know the course of fate;
the future is known to God alone. Yet despair   500
is a sin; hard labor will make our wishes come true.
Our art is vigilance; it will bear fruit.
Hope and labor are subject to fickle chance,[9]
but hope itself increases with a good beginning.

15

PAMPHILUS: Can you tell if she loves me or not?   505
Love has trouble keeping its secrets.

BAWD: When I talked to her, she hung on my every word,
so sweet were the words I was saying.
Putting her arms around my shoulders,
she asked the message you had sent her;   510
and when in the course of our talk I came to pronounce
your name, she was overcome by emotion.
Joyful at my words, she kept blushing, then growing pale.
And when tired of talking I fell silent, she urged me to speak on.
By these and other signs we know she loves,   515
nor did she deny she's your true friend.

PAMPHILUS: Now success is at hand, thanks to your labor!
Glory flourishes, with your aid!
Sometimes only persistence resolves our doubts.
Work on, work quickly, hasten this undertaking,
and don't delay; any laziness will lose our advantage.   520
As much as you can, hasten to complete the task
you've begun; don't let lazy delay do harm.

BAWD: I know that you will get everything you want;
my only doubt regards your promises to me.
Our intentions often contradict our words,   525
nor do we always do what we say.
Unkept promises debase the purchased labor.
Perhaps when you're happy, you won't give me a thing.

PAMPHILUS: It is a terrible crime for a rich man
to cheat the poor; if I should cheat you,
what honor would I have then?   530
Neither you, not anyone, have I ever betrayed,
and if you inquire, you'll find my reputation spotless.
You have my word. You can be utterly confident;
you need have no fear.

BAWD: Humble folk must always fear   535
to fall victim to the cleverness of the mighty.
The laws offer the poor man but little protection,

16

and nowadays, good faith is despoiled of former status.
She is hidden by countless webs of crime.
One must not, however, question fate.
The sea that seems frightening may not be dangerous.   540
So I trust to Fortune for the reward you've promised me,
and you can be sure that you will get
the reward that I've promised you.
Now, I must go and entreat Galathea
to come alone to talk with you here.
If my guile brings the two of you together,   545
while you have the chance, I pray you, be a man!
The lover's heart and mind are always inconstant;
a brief instant will give you what you seek.

A great blaze cannot hide its light, nor Venus her desires.   550
I know everything that has passed between you;
when I think of it, I can scarce keep from crying.
I see clearly that you love beyond reason;
your folly is its own betrayer.
A pale face reveals a secret love; you are wasting away,   555
and not from hard work either.

[*to Galathea*]

Pamphilus, poor Pamphilus, he is always so miserable;
his looks reveal how harshly you've treated him.
Day and night he labors in love like a silly boy,
but the ungrateful fields give him nothing in return.   560
Who, if he were not beyond reason,
would sow his seed in sterile sand?
Work is more pleasant if it enjoys some hope of reward.
First your beauty, then your words betrayed him;
with these two weapons love has wounded him most sorely,
nor have you brought him the cure you promised.   565
Now his grief afflicts him worse than his hope;
now his wounds lack salve; his pain exceeds all bounds.
And though you keep silent, the flames may burn you too!
Unconfessed hurts breed suffering and death;
love concealed and denied only grows worse.   570
Therefore, consider quickly what you want to do

17

and let me know of your intentions.

GALATHEA: Venus the cruel oppresses me with burning thoughts;
doing me violence, she continually orders me to love.
Yet modesty and fear bid me to be chaste. 575
With such compelling arguments on both sides
I don't know what to do.

BAWD: Let fear keep its distance! There is no cause for fear.
There will be no betrayer in this affair.
Pamphilus wishes only to be yours;
all his care and his labor strive only for this. 580
In a thousand ways his looks reveal the fires burning him.
Weeping bitterly, he said to me,
"Galathea is my cause for grief and my cure;
she is the only one who can injure or save me."
Pity made me weep with him, 585
but in the depths of my heart I was glad.
I saw that everything was going just as I wished;
I saw that you both burn with equal and painful desire.
Those flames usually do harm; spare yourselves.
Love can unite you, with my aid. 590

GALATHEA: That which you seek I also want,
but it would be dearer to me if my parents consented.
It is not proper for me alone to dare do this,
and even if I were willing, I would have no chance.
Mother always keeps a guardian with me; 595
the whole house watches me, day and night.

BAWD: Love the clever can open doors and undo locks,
conquering whatever gets in its way, oh clever Love.
Set aside vain fear; forget your childish worries.
Sweet love calls you — come with me. 600

GALATHEA: You now share the secrets of my heart;
indeed, you are my better part, and I beg you,
give me good advice, advice you're not ashamed to give.
It is a shame and a crime to seduce girls by treachery; 605
this affair can lead to great honor or great sin.[10]

BAWD: I am not ashamed!
I'll not hide my head before the gossiping crowd!
I'll not deny having advised you!
If anyone wishes to oppose me in this,
let him summon all the objections he can. 610
Let him assemble all his forces and do battle with me.
If conquered, let him keep silent,
or quickly let him emerge victorious.
How easily Reason and I will check him,
since he can say nothing reasonable against me.
    Pamphilus is a good man, and handsome too, 615
nobly born, wealthy — sweet love will be our accomplice.
Chattering Rumor will keep silent, silent too all evil whispers.
You may go your way without shame.

GALATHEA: O God! with what indecision is a lover's heart torn;
fear pulls it one way, great love the other. 620
These two enemies assail me day and night.
Love says "Yes," and fear says "No."
I wander, lost in the wilderness.
Love's wound grows worse, lost as I am.
Love subdues me even though I resist it constantly. 625
Love assails me the more fiercely the more I resist it.
I have suffered so long that I tremble, exhausted by travail,
and sad to say, I'd rather die than live.

BAWD: Just as flames grow hotter when fanning,
and quarrels and anger increase with resistance, 630
so Venus herself is hurt by her own warfare,
and opposition only makes things worse.
You cannot put out your passionate fires by making war on them;
love's peace will cool the painful flames.
Obey the orders of Venus while you are under her command, 635
lest your resistance do you harm. Be bold! Go forward!
You would be wrong to let life's joys escape you;
you would always regret your mistake.
    You seem content to ponder the face of your absent lover,
just as he, night and day, thinks of yours; 640
but if you persist in gazing on faces only,
delay will be the death of you both.

19

Are you perhaps planning to reject this man
whom you love but casually? His death will be the result.
Don't punish your youth; embrace life's joys!   645
It is right to feed a cheerful heart on cheerful sport.
    You are alone at the moment;
come to my house and enjoy yourself awhile.
    See, Galathea, at my house there are apples and nuts for you.
My garden is hardly ever without fruit;
look, you can enjoy whatever you wish.   650
               [*a knocking is heard*]
    But now someone — I don't know who it is — bangs at my door.
Was it a man or was it the wind?
I think it was a man. It is a man!
He's looking in at us through a crack.
It's Pamphilus! I recognize his face.
By skill and by force, little by little,   655
he's pulling back the bolt on the door.
He's coming in. Does he think
I'll stand for this without a word?
    Why so furiously break down my door, Pamphilus?
You've broken the new bolt that I just bought.
What do you want? Have you a message for us?
If you have something to say, say it quickly and get out!   660

PAMPHILUS: O Galathea, my only hope of salvation!
After such long delays, give me a thousand kisses;
               [*he kisses her*]
But my thirsty ardor is unquenched, unsatisfied by kisses;
it grows hotter, fed by such mild pleasures.
Look, I embrace all my joys;   665
I hold in my hands a sweet and sacred burden.
What happy chance directed my footsteps here?
This place contains all that I love best.

BAWD: I hear my neighbor calling me;
I'll go talk to her, then come right back,
for I very much fear she's going to come over here.   670
          [*to the neighbor, offstage*]
What's that you're shouting? I'm coming as quick as I can.
I'm just going to close the door

since there's no one home; the house is empty.
I am busy; come and tell me quickly what you want;
my business will brook no delay.

[*exit the Bawd*]

PAMPHILUS: Look how sweet love, blooming youth, and opportunity   675
all urge us, Galathea, to feed our hearts with sport.
Lascivious Venus compels us to taste her joys,
orders us now to go on. Why do I delay?
Shall I, a suppliant, seek her aid for my desires?
I beg you now, be obedient to my will.   680

GALATHEA: Pamphilus, take your hands off me!
You are wearing yourself out in vain!
This labor won't get you anywhere!
What you want cannot be!
Pamphilus, take your hands off!
Alas, how little strength we women have;   685
how easily you hold fast my hands!
Pamphilus, you're hurting my breasts with your breast.
Why are you treating me like this?
It is a crime and a sin!
Stop it! I'll scream.
What are you doing?
It is wrong to take my clothes off!
Oh poor me, when will that treacherous woman return?   690
Get off, I beg you. The neighbors will hear!
She did wrong, that old woman, entrusting me to you.
I'll never come here again;
she will not deceive me a second time.
        You've conquered me, however strongly I resisted,   695
but all hope of love is shattered between us — forever!

PAMPHILUS: Now then, we should both rest a bit,
as when a horse, his race completed, breathes deeply.
Why don't you look at your beloved?
Why is your face covered with tears?   700
I am wholly at fault; I'll accept
whatever punishment you devise,

21

though it be greater than I deserve.
Look, I am content to submit to any punishment you wish.
Still, it wasn't my fault that I sinned.
If you prefer, let us submit our case to impartial justice;   705
either I go free or am condemned in the court of Reason.
Your passionate eyes, your fair skin, your youthful face,
embraces, sweet kisses, flirtations —
these were my incitements to crime!
These were the first cause of my sin.
With such encouragement, love absolutely insisted;   710
my madness swelled; the heat of lust burned like a frenzy.
Your charms drove me to do this sinful deed.
That most vile error overthrew my reason,
making pity deaf to your entreaties.
But for those crimes of which I stand accused,   715
it is rightly you who are guilty;
you were the inspiration, the first cause of this sin.
       It isn't right for such a serious quarrel to go on
between two lovers, but since it has come up,
pray, let's be certain it is brief.
A lover must always forgive her beloved's faults.   720
Bear patiently our mutual guilt.
When the old woman returns, I beg you, look happy
lest she discover our fault through your tears.

BAWD: That woman kept me outside with her empty chatter —
she'd outdo Cicero himself for longwindedness.
Why, Galathea, why are your eyes full of tears?   725
This blushing I see so plainly, what is its cause?
When I was gone, did Pamphilus do anything to you?
I beg you, Galathea, tell me the whole story.

GALATHEA: It suits you, doesn't it, to pretend
that you have no idea what happened,
when everything was done in accord with your plans.   730
As a tree is known by its fruit,
so you will be known by your deeds.
Apples and nuts — you were deceitful to offer me them
when that Pamphilus of yours was right at your door.
And your neighbor, she called you   735

22

so that he would have the opportunity for this,
for me to lose my virginity.
What else caused you to delay so long out of doors?
How well your art concealed your snares.
Your art and deceit have run their course;
the fleeting hare has fallen into your trap.   740

BAWD: I am unjustly accused. Away with all blame for me!
I shall clear myself to your satisfaction.
This accusation does not accord well with my years,
nor do I employ my skill in such evil ways.
If some quarrel arose in your play,   745
how could I be at fault?
I was not even here! Be that as it may,
this strife has nothing to do with me.
It wasn't I but your love which inspired it.
Nevertheless, Pamphilus, tell me, in order,
all the things of which I am ignorant;
I must know the origin of all this trouble.   750

PAMPHILUS: I am accused of a mere trifle,
if you would know the whole story.
Her anger is far greater than I deserve.
But lovers ought to keep their secrets;
it is a shame to speak of such things
when in fact nothing shameful took place.
                  [*to Galathea*]
You must lay aside this lovers' quarrel;   755
what happened between us concerns us only.

GALATHEA: Pamphilus, tell her what really happened,
just as if she did not know,
just as if she had not instigated the whole plan.
Feigning ignorance, she asks you,
she who told you just what to do,
so she won't seem the one who betrayed me.   760
By countless arts you have led me astray,
but your guileful art informs upon itself.
Too late the fish, already caught, feels the hook;
too late the bird, already caught, sees the snare.

Pamphilus

But now, what am I to do?   765
Am I to flee through the world, already caught?[11]
My parents will be right to close the door on me.
I shall wander the earth, searching,
but nowhere shall I find happiness,
poor betrayed wretch that I am.

BAWD: The wise do not indulge in immoderate grief,
since grief brings no reward to its master.   770
Accept calmly those things which art cannot repair,
which unrestrained love has evilly wrought.
Moderation and prudence, that's what our case requires.
Seek out the best course of action.
Painful discord consumes the hearts of lovers   775
and nourishes blind wounds with its battles.
Make peace now; it's the best for your both.
Let this woman be your wife.
Let this man be your husband.
Through my aid, you both now have what you wanted;
through me you are happy. Never forget me!   780

Notes to *Pamphilus*

1. Text taken from the edition of Evesque in Cohen, II, pp. 194-223, but taking into account the more recent critical edition of Pittaluga.

2. Keeping silent about one's love is one of the most common medieval tenets on love. Pamphilus' further remarks, however, indicate that he has more practical considerations in mind.

3. Compare Vergil, *Georgics* 1.145-46, "labor omnia vicit improbus" (*Pamph.*, "labor improbus omnia vincit"). *Improbus*, which means both "persistent" and "bold," "excessive," is a stock epithet for love (e.g. *Aeneid* 4.412, "Improbe Amor, quid non mortalia pectore cogis," Bold love, to what do you not drive mortal hearts). After this Vergilian quotation, however, the rest of the speech is a mosaic of citations from the first book of the *Ars Amatoria*.

4. A reference to *Ars Amatoria* 1.663.

5. In some manuscripts this speech is given to Pamphilus.

6. *Thus*, sic, *seems* to indicate that a gesture is to accompany the words, yet another indication of the theatricality of *Pamphilus*.

7. The popular handbook of wise sayings, the *Distichs of Cato* (2.27), advised that it was the height of prudence to assume the guise of folly.

8. As Bate notes (p. 75), this line parodies the Palm Sunday hymn attributed to Theodulf of Orléans, *Gloria, laus et honor tibi sit, rex Christe, redemptor* (Glory, praise and honor be thine, king Christ, redeemer).

9. In some MSS lines 503-504 are given to Pamphilus.

10. In some MSS these two lines are given to the Bawd.

11. *Captiva* "captured": the Latin here is influenced by the French *chétive*, "wretched."

GETA[1]

by Vitalis of Blois

ARGUMENT

Pursuing his study of the Greeks long and hard,
Amphitryon was absent from home,
and Geta went with him to be his companion.
In disguise Saturn's son gains entrance
to Alcmena; his companion was Archas.
She thought him her husband. At long last
Geta returns, sent on ahead by Amphitryon.   5
Archas tricks him into believing
that he is nothing; unhappy at being nothing
Geta departs, deceived by Archas,
and tells his master what he has seen.
The husband grieves and readies his arms.
Satisfied, the father of the gods departs,
and Archas with him. The others seek the lecher;
he is not to be found. They rejoice,
their quarrel is settled, their anger cools.   10

PROLOGUE

In writing these verses the poet wished
to give pleasure; his desire deceived him.
No poem, no tale, gives pleasure;
everyone seeks only serious things.
The immoderate love of possessions binds
fast the whole world. Love of wealth
is triumphant, and poetry must give way before money.   15
You can be just as wise as you like;
if you have no money, you're nobody.
Even if someone really is pleased
by a literary work, he still bears it
ill-will and, praising the ancient authors,
does not know how to enjoy the modern.
It would have been far more practical

26

to have kept silent, not written verse,
for there is no reward for the writer,   20
there is no praise for the poem.
If a man enjoys this sort of work,
let him scribble away for himself,
let him think that he is grand —
he'll be the only one to love his creation.

THE TALE

Saturn's son burns for Alcmena and,
thinking how blessed was Amphitryon,
grieves to be Jove. "What," he says,
"shall not the race of the gods take pride   25
in Jove their father? At this very moment
the gods' father is less than Amphitryon."

The caduceus-bearer had gone to greet his father
(he was his messenger). "You've come,"
says Jupiter, "just when I want you.
I burn for Alcmena, but nonetheless
I do not enflame her, only myself.
Her husband is conveniently absent;   30
I shall enjoy his place.
Let Jupiter study in Alcmena's bedroom,
her husband philosophize in Athens.
Let Jupiter love, Amphitryon read;
let Amphitryon dispute, and Jove deceive.
Let him cherish the liberal arts —
Jupiter will cherish his Alcmena.
But already Amphitryon prepares to return;   35
therefore, I beg you, dress up as Geta.
Your father will be Amphitryon."

The gods endured to assume mortal guise;
the father becomes Amphitryon, his son is Geta.
Gossip, inspired by multiple rumors,
announces to Alcmena her husband's return.
The news gives her great joy. She orders   40
the household to rejoice at her lord's return;

27

she decks the halls with ivory, the bed with broad purple.
The bedroom smiles and glows, laden with gold.
She brings the wealth of absent Amphitryon
out from hiding. By her joy, her beauty,
and her festive clothing, she tells the house   45
of her husband's return. Her hair is artfully
arranged, her right hand proudly wears gold,
and she paints her face so that art
might enhance her natural beauty.
Thus she surpasses all other women,
thus she surpasses even herself.
She becomes someone new and even more fair,   50
and even more pleasing to Jove.

      "Go now, my boy," cries Saturn's son.
"Come on! Just look at Alcmena,
how good, how beautiful, how very much better
than that Juno of mine!
Alcmena vanquishes my constellations,
outshines the stars, overshadows the day.
Thus she pleases me; let her come out   55
like this to greet me, and let her submit
to Jove in Amphitryon's place."

      They leave heaven. The earth gives off the fragrance
of gentle spring, sensing the presence of gods.
Let Alcmena rejoice. Her husband's at hand.
See how the rumor grows, swearing the fleet has returned.   60

      "Look, my Amphitryon has come back!
Quickly, Birria,[2] get up!" Alcmena had spoken.[3]
She cries out; the other keeps silent.
Birria says to himself, "Let her
shout all she likes, you keep quiet.
Let her be wide awake, you sleep.
Let her run about, you lie still.
Let games and hard work keep the others busy;
Birria, sleep's your occupation.   65
Others may do just as they like —
this is the right job for you."

Then Alcmena repeats, "Hurry, Birria, get up!"
Her entreaties did her no good.
She added threats; her threats he obeyed.
His mistress tells him, "Go to the shore,
take note of the sails, look for ships;   70
report what you've seen, and tell the truth,
so that I may know whether the rumor
about Amphitryon's return is true or not.
And oh, I pray, let it be true, not false!"
    This was what the mistress said,
and this what the servant replied:
"Alas, poor Birria, that's a tall order.
Why, the sea's waves terrify even the bold.
When I stand on the shore, I shall take   75
good care lest the waves as they ebb
pull me in headlong. If you fell in,
Birria, there'd be no one to weep for you.
Why, what would Amphitryon say?
'Birria was nobody,' that's what he'd say.
Oh, my poor feet, my poor sides! The road
is rough. It's a long way to the ships.   80
I'm going, never more to return.
Whether I come back or not, Alcmena, listen:
if Amphitryon's going to return,
he'll return when he's good and ready."

    Angrily redoubling her threats, she
gives the order. "I'm going," he says,
"but pray to the gods, I beg you,
for my safe return." He goes; she prays.
"Be with me, good Jupiter," she says.   85

Archas, pretending he's Geta, answers her,
saying, "Here he is!"

One god enters as Geta, as Amphitryon
the other. "Hail, Alcmena," Jupiter says,
triumphant. "And Amphitryon, hail,"
rejoins Alcmena. They multiply kisses;
they give, then repeat the giving.   90

29

Alcmena is self-controlled, and her
delightful kisses are restrained;
womanly modesty governs her speech.
But the god, he's more wanton.
Pressing her mouth hard, with his
tongue he caresses, his lips opened wide.
His kisses savor of unrestrained passion;
his words were those of Jove.

    She hangs from Jupiter's neck, her weight   95
a welcome burden to the god's neck,
for this was how he loved to be burdened.
"I could not be happier," she says,
"if I embraced Jupiter himself,"
comparing the god to his very self.
Their kisses mingle.
By now Jupiter burns even hotter.
"Shut the doors, Geta," he says,   100
"and make fast the bolt. If sailors come
drive away all that brutal tribe.
Let no one approach the gates;
let the door cling lovingly to its sill.
Let a more intimate chamber receive us."
Archas is willing. The room receives them.
He bolts the door.
The room's very appearance invites
each of them to embraces.
Delay displeases; the bed unites them.   105

    Birria slowly goes on his way,
limping along, bitterly complaining
of the road's roughness, making the
road the cause of his sluggish pace.
"Woe is me," said he. "The length
of this road will wear out my feet.   110
I was born for ill, to be tortured
while everyone else is resting quietly.
Woe to a man, whoever he is,
who must obey a woman's commands.
A woman wants her servants to sweat;

she has learned how to give orders.
Hardship binds the servants fast
while she attends to her complexion.
Just so that her lover can enter, she makes   115
up the tale that her husband's returned.
And lest you see that lover, Birria,
you're driven out. Should I go home
and complain of her actions?
When I've caught her out, she'll be afraid,
and being afraid, she'll have to restrain
her blows, her scoldings and threats."
So he speaks and turns back.
Then he hesitates, reconsiders,
stops, and speaks once again to himself: 120
"I'm acting unwisely. Crime breeds courage.
If I catch her out, she'll really hate me.
Whatever Birria does, he'll always be in the wrong.
Husbands are always credulous, believing their wives.
That wicked woman will have me condemned
for some pretended crime. I'll pay
on the gallows for what I've witnessed.
I must resume my appointed task.   125
The job is urgent; I've got to get going,
but, Birria, be sure that you take a roundabout route. That road, take that one,
so you don't meet Geta who'll break your back
with some deadly burden or other.
May Geta perish, that's my prayer,
a man born to bear burdens. Let a horse   130
bear the load, and Birria live like a man."

    Having safely escaped wind and water,
Amphitryon happily entered the harbor
and Geta with him. A chaste love
for his wife reigns in his heart.
He called and Geta approaches.
"Go quickly," he told him. "Take my books   135
and run on ahead. Greet Alcmena;
let her rejoice that I've returned.
Half of me now is safe; may the other

31

half be so, I pray. All my safety depends on her."

     Geta agrees and takes up the books;
he goes, the advance messenger.
Birria is en route; he sees Geta.   140
"Alas, that's Geta," he says; "now I've had it!
Just what I feared has happened. Alas,
what a burden he bears and how well!
Great Atlas himself would sweat under that load,
and it's going to be placed on my shoulders.
Look, here's a cave. Let me hide there   145
until he's passed; then I'll go my way."
He finished his speech and hid. But Geta,
who knew him well, sees him first.
He marks where Birria is hiding,
though pretends not to notice. He stops
by the cave; resting his burden
on a two-pronged stick, he speaks   150
to himself like this: "Oh, my poor arms,
poor shoulders, I'm so weighted down!
The weight wears my back out, the road my feet.
But why doesn't Birria run out to meet Geta?
Then he could carry my burden on his back;
then Birria would be the one to stumble along   155
beneath this bundle."

                Birria says to himself:
"That was a good idea of yours to hide!"

     Geta continues: "Woe, woe is me,"
he said. "It would take forever
to tell all the evils I've had to suffer
in Athens — cold, continual hunger,
fierce thirst, far too little sleep,   160
wretched food — they've all done me in.
My master lives on second-rate bread;
that which feeds me is barely fourth-rate.[4]
But as a reward for my pains I'm bringing back
some really amazing sophistries, for I know
how to prove that a man is an ass.

When I'm back home among the pots and pans,   165
deep in the greasy kitchen,
I shall prove that some men are asses
while others are cows. I'm a logician!
I shall make everyone into whatever
animal I please. Old Birria,
since he's so slow, shall be an ass."

       Birria says to himself, "What,
Birria become an ass! Can he take away   170
what nature has given? Whatever enigmas
Geta may pose, Birria will answer
Geta like this: 'Birria will always be a MAN.'"

[GETA] "I also have learned this lesson,
that matter can never perish;
once something exists, it can never be nothing.
He to whom existence is once granted   175
is never allowed not to exist;
he merely changes his aspect and renews
his essence. Therefore I can never
be nothing."

       Then Birria says to himself,
"Geta will live forever, if he's telling the truth."

[GETA] "Death bears everything away.
They say that Plato the wise has fallen,
and Socrates himself been struck down.   180
My reputation will live, but even this
death too will overthrow. Death
destroys all; by death all are brought low."

[BIRRIA] "He's disagreeing with himself.
Just a moment ago he was proving
that everything lacked an ending;
now he grieves that death puts an end to all."

[GETA] "Well, I'm on my way. But wait,   185
what's rustling there, murmuring deep

33

down in the grotto? Look, a rabbit!
By god, a fine prey for a man.
I'll use these rocks, for I don't have my net.
My forked stick will serve as a net,
and the rocks will do for the dogs.
Just let him try to run out or hide;
my rocks will get him; this prey I've found   190
will do nicely to enrich my table."

[BIRRIA] "Woe is me! Why did I hide?
I wanted to escape death; now I'm dying.
I wanted to live; now my life's escaping.
Oh, I was too concerned about being safe;
now I shall be hidden forever,
and this cavern will be my grave.
Oh, why didn't I keep quiet?   195
Now I've betrayed myself; now I fear
I'm going to die. I was good and safe."

    Geta takes his stones and rains down blow
upon blow. In a timid voice Birria
begs for mercy. "I'm Birria.
My Geta, I beg you, spare me, your friend.
There's no glory for a man, stoning   200
his mate like this. Geta, stay your hand.
It's me, Birria, in here."

                "You're not
Birria," Geta responds. Birria swears he is,
and Geta denies it.
One utters threats, the other cries out.

[BIRRIA] "I'm not lying, by God! You know me,
you can recognize me by my voice.
I'm Birria. Geta, put down the stones,
so Birria may live to serve you."   205

[GETA] "Then stick out your head."

[BIRRIA] "I'm sticking it out. Put the stones down

so you don't hurt my head with them.' "

The one stops; the other emerges.
Geta addresses him: "Why were you hiding?
Someone who wasn't as careful as I am   210
could have made you suffer a terrible death."

[BIRRIA] "Who gave Geta the right to stone
anyone who is hiding? The moon
hides when she wishes, Birria when he can."

[GETA] "Run quickly to the ships and gather
all the baggage remaining. There's a heavy load
just waiting for your shoulders, or, if you prefer,   215
there's this itty, bitty burden of mine."

[BIRRIA] "Itty bitty! Who could carry
such a weight?"

[GETA]   "Oh, you'll carry
a bigger one; its bulk will squash you."
And showing his bundle of books, he says,
"This is very light weight."

[BIRRIA] "Since you complain that you're carrying
a light weight, or else none at all,
why don't you carry this light one;
it's just about right for your strength."   220

[GETA] "When I wanted to carry the biggest,
Amphitryon said to me, 'Geta,
you will take this light one. Let Birria
bear the big one, for rest has made him
strong; big burdens suit strong shoulders.'"

[BIRRIA] "Birria will be forced to move mountains."   225

[GETA] "Then take mine."

[BIRRIA]   "You keep the load

35

that you have; if I can't escape,
at least I can postpone my hard labor."

    They separate. One seeks the harbor,
the other heads straight for the house.
Geta hurries home rejoicing
to see familiar places. To make the journey   230
seem shorter he counts his blessings:
"Rejoice, Geta, your labors are over.
Repose has returned; peace and quiet
will now be your lot. Samnio, Sanga,
and Davus[5] will stand up to welcome Geta,
and the rest of the crowd will applaud their pal.
My name will grow longer. I'll be called   235
MASTER GETA. My name's very shadow
will strike terror in all.
I'll be GETA THE GREAT, venerated
by the whole kitchen crew.
I'll teach my servants great things.
    "But why doesn't Alcmena come out to greet us?
What, is the door closed to me?   240
Does the house remain silent? The door
will fly open at Geta's first word;
with my little finger I'll unbolt the gates.
I bring trinkets a woman finds pleasing;
there's a peplum for Alcmena, a belt,
a necklace, and a Greek cloak.
Elegance enhances beauty.   245
A woman can be proud with such treasure;
with it she is pleasing to her husband,
but more pleasing, by far, to herself."

    He approaches and knocks on the door.
The silence of the house, shut tight,
dumbfounds him. His voice fills the courtyard.
"Let Alcmena come out! Throw open the doors
wide for Geta. Let her come out and see   250
her Amphitryon."

        Archas appears at the door,

disguised as Geta. He resembles him closely
in face and body, more closely in voice.

[ARCHAS] "Amphitryon holds sway already
in the bedroom; Geta guards the gates.
Whoever you are, go away." He finished speaking.
The other stands speechless;
the disguised voice terrified⁶ Geta.   255
He draws back from the doors and sadly he says,
"That man who spoke to me,
in voice and in name, he's Geta;
but who can speak with Geta's words
except Geta? Logicians, however, teach us
that one word will be used for two
quite different objects, and two   260
people will have the same name."

    He finished his speech. He looks at the house
closed up tight on all sides;
he sees everything shut and silent.
Amazed, he stands before the doors and shouts,
"Whoever you are, open the gates.
Unlock the doors. Geta's come home."

[ARCHAS] "Geta's already home," the god says,   265
"and Amphitryon is enjoying himself
in his wife's bed. Birria has also
returned — poor Birria, who while he lay
hidden away in a grotto was terrified
by threats and by rocks someone threw.
Stop your shouting. Let tired men sleep.
Sleep's the more pleasing to those exhausted   270
by toil. Geta knows his name,
but Geta won't open the closed door
to you at the mere sound of the name Geta."

    Geta was stunned and retreated again,
saying, "Woe is me. He's the real Geta.
His voice and his deeds prove it.
Have I gone astray somewhere? Has Birria,   275

37

whom I just sent packing, already returned
faster than I or by some shorter route?
I'm talking to myself but I don't know how
we've become two; formerly we were but one.
Everything that exists is unique,
but I who am speaking am not unique:
therefore it follows that Geta is nothing.   280
But he can't be nothing. I was unique
when I first addressed that closed door,
but he made me answer myself.
Did I do that? Or did the house
just echo my voice, as often happens in the forest?
That door, once thrown open, used to receive me,   285
I who am begging to enter today — oh, it's madness!
I will approach him, will ask him
all about his feet, his teeth, his hair —
whether he's me in body as well
as in voice. I will inquire
all about his deeds, his morals.
It's no trifling fear to think   290
that Geta is either double or nothing!"

    He approaches; to break the bolts
barring his way he bangs on the shut door
with an angry fist. He cries out,
"Are you there, you with Geta's name
and his voice? Unbolt the door,
it's shut tight, I beg you,
so that I can see — I'm not asking   295
to come in — just to look
through the half-opened door[7] to see
if your features are also like mine."

    "No," Archas answers him, "it's not
that easy to deceive Geta.
If you can't get in by force,
you're prepared to try guile."

    Geta requests; Archas denies.
Geta attacks; Archas repels.

They come to blows but Archas is stronger.   300
Their insults mingle together, and
leaning against the doorposts, peevishly
they hurl empty threats back and forth.

    Geta screams, "If you don't pull
back the bolt of your own free will,
you vile creature, you'll feel my strength,
by Hercules! Unbar that door,   305
you impudent scoundrel! If you don't
open it at once, I'll break it down,
right now, with my club. It's shameful
for me to beg when I could compel.
Alcmena, what are you doing? Get up!
Open the house. Oh, it's disgraceful
for a wife not to run out to greet
her husband when he returns home.   310
Look, your Geta is here on the doorstep.
Look, your Amphitryon too, he's here.
Quickly order the bolts drawn back.
This jailbird here won't let Geta in."

    "If you try some dirty trick,"
Archas says, "may the gods above
strike me dead if you don't discover
what sort of stuff Geta is made of."

[BIRRIA] "I'll break the door down with my club!"   315

[ARCHAS] "And I will break your neck.
Stop your terrible, bellowing roars.
Do you think you can scare me with threats?
Any injury to that door will rebound
painfully, by god, on your head."

    Geta is frightened; he stops his threats.
Cheated of threats' support, Geta returns   320
to his usual form of address — he begs.
"Tell me," he says, "I pray you, your features,
what are they like, what color's your skin?

39

Add a description of all your limbs;
go over each particular, for I need to know
whether anyone, except me, can be me."

      Archas replies, "Well, I'll tell you,   325
since you beg me, for I can be swayed
by entreaties but not by threats.
First of all, to be really wise,
you must stop believing that you are Geta.
I don't imagine that you really do
believe it; just believe me instead.
Greece knows no other Geta but me;
indeed you sought to cheat me of my name.   330
I'm the one and only Geta!
Now learn about my complexion, my build,
how each separate member is fashioned.
      "I am wholly condemned to an outlandish,
villainous black hue; my whole body's
the same color. I resemble an Ethiop
or one in India born and bred.   335
My black skin is always disfigured
by running sores. My head is hairy,
my hair like a goat's; my forehead is low,
my nose is long, my eyes are red.
A forest of hairs quite overshadows
my chin and cheeks. My neck is scrawny,   340
my shoulders narrow, my stomach so swollen
they call me hydropic; my stomach knows nothing
at all of moderation or measure.
No belt can chastise this swelling
when my paunch is puffed out by bread
soaked in water. There's not room enough
for my sides, for my loins.   345
I have hairy thighs and the itch
reigns there as king. And when with frequent
palpitation my prick gathers its ire,
it extends to my knees — and that's a long way,
as my knees are very close to the ground.
My shanks are short and stout, my feet
so crooked no sandal will fit them.   350

Everyone finds it enough to meet me
just once; when they see me coming
all fastidious natures depart,
nor do they say *au revoir.*"

      Geta is amazed; he sees and hears
his very description: "Whoever he is,
he is Geta; I'm just like that," he says.
"Then tell me how, by what guile,   355
have you deceived Amphitryon, so that
by deeds as well you may be me and I nothing?"

      "Listen, then, to the tale of my tricks
and my wiles," the caduceus-bearer replies,
"so that you can swear that I
am Geta and you're a mere nothing.
Though I am a disgrace, there is a woman
who has enjoyed being loved by Geta.
Do you know why? She's a disgrace too!   360
But there's an even better reason: I'm insatiable.
Priapus' madness always burns hotly within me,
and my measure knows no moderation.
To tell the truth, it's not
Geta she loves but his groin.
If she's not fond of my face, there are
parts of me that please her better.
Those whom my face makes my enemies,   365
another part makes friends of mine.
Therefore one part makes me loved as a whole.
      "I deceive my old man. I steal
part of what he's entrusted to me;
I steal hidden things, and feed my Thais
on furtive goods. No lock stops Geta's hands.
I'm prodigal; I dissipate everything.
I'm very generous — with others' goods.   370
I pacify with presents those my face frightens.
If you have much to give, you can have
whatever you want. Listen now
to what I just did in Athens.
You'll have to admit that my deeds

41

prove that I'm Geta. Amphitryon
has his studies, and Geta his Thais.   375
When I change countries, I seek a new Thais,
and a goodly number of them seek me out.
I conquer with gifts. Generous love is victorious.
And when my master is weighed down by slumber,
I chastise his proud purse, diminish
its contents, so it is less puffed up.   380
Often have I deserved to be hanged,
even more often deserved to be fettered.
Often have I endured whippings and threats.
Why, just recently — but come here,
I don't want anyone else to hear this terrible secret —
I took two talents out of the strongbox
without damaging it; I had made
a duplicate key to conceal my theft.   385
It's an easy job to deceive foolish old men.
But if my deceit fails and I'm caught
in the act, I deny the obvious.
I call on the heavenly powers, I swear
by the gods. I don't hesitate
to add the gods as false witnesses.
No man dares to do great deeds   390
if he believes that the gods exist."

      "That's enough, you're Geta," Geta replies.
He recognizes the tale and grieves
to know that it's common knowledge.
"Henceforth you can be me," he answers;
"let me be nothing." He departs, going
back down the road which just now,
in a happier mood, he had come up.

      He departs alone. He complains   395
to himself: "Woe, woe is me," he says.
"Woe to me who once existed
but who now have become nothing.
Geta, who in the world can you be?
You are a man. No, by god,
for if Geta's a man, who can

he be if not Geta? I'm Plato!
Perhaps my studies have made me Plato.
I'm certainly not Geta though Geta I'm called.
If I'm not Geta, they shouldn't call me that.   400
I used to be called Geta, but what
will my name be now? I will have no name
since I am nothing. Alas, I am nothing.
Now I speak and see; I touch my hand."
Touching his hand, he draws the following   405
inference: "By Hercules, I am touched!
Whatever is tangible cannot be nothing.
Whatever has been continues to be; it does not
cease being. He exists always to whom
existence is once given.
Therefore I am; therefore I am not.
Oh, damnation to this dialectic
which has condemned me utterly to non-existence.
Now I have knowledge, but knowledge is dangerous.   410
When Geta learned logic he ceased to exist.
Logic, which changes others into cows,
has changed me into nothing.
Its sophisms have dealt me the cruelest
of blows. Others it merely transforms;
from me it has taken my essence. A curse
on all logic if that's what it does.   415
         "Alas, here comes Amphitryon.
I wonder whether he too is nothing.
Can that which is nothing approach?
By Hercules, everything is out of line!
I was a fool; dialectic made me mad.
But Geta can prove whether he still exists: 420
I do if he salutes me as Geta. If he's silent,
well, then, I've had it for sure."
He finished⁸ his speech and quickly goes forward.

         Amphitryon is returning. Birria,
following him, staggers along,
groaning under a very light load.
When Amphitryon sees Geta he says,   425
"By great Jupiter, what does Geta want?

43

Why has he returned? Does his swift return
portend some loss? Dear Juno,
make him the bearer of good news.
Let him not bring me news of the death
of a child, the death of my wife
from disease. I'm frightened.   430
He looks sorrowful; I am disturbed
by his appearance. Grant, oh powers above,
that I not be told that I am without heirs,
or that death has taken away
a great part of my existence.
Why am I silent? I shall ask him."
Thus he speaks, and seizing him says,
"Tell me, come on, Geta, how does
my true love fare? Do we stand or fall?
Has death taken my faithful wife?   435
Does my love live?"

                To his questions
Geta replies, "By Hercules,
I really am Geta; he called me by name.
That which is nothing can't have a name."
These things he thinks to himself, then adds,
"By Hercules, I have incredible news.   440
We've both been home a long time.
By Hercules, we are not here.
Birria has also returned already,
and Amphitryon is master
of the bedroom and Geta of the gate.
What I'm telling you is really true,
alas, all too true! I'd be very happy
if I were telling you a pack of lies.
Assuming that you really are Amphitryon,   445
you sent me off. I departed
and found the gate bolted fast.
I banged loudly on the doors.
Geta ordered me out and proved
beyond any doubt that Amphitryon
had already returned to his home.
He described me to myself;

44

he knew all my deeds and convinced me
by countless proofs that he was Geta."   450

     Birria laughs and says, "Greece
received them sane but sent them home
insane. Dialectic makes all fools
lose their senses. Birria, don't let yourself
ever learn an art like that one.
It's good to be ignorant of an art   455
which by some fancy makes men
into asses or else into nothing.
Let everyone else turn logician, but you,
Birria, always remain a man!
Let logicians delight in scholarship
if they like; the greasy kitchen
is the proper study for you."

     Geta tells his tale; he can't
believe himself; he's still amazed.

     Anxiety grips Amphitryon.   460
"You've been deceived," Amphitryon says,
"because of your fear of being nothing.
There must have been an adulterer
in her bedroom, one to whom
you were well-known. Give me my armor.
Geta, gird on a sword. Birria,
grab your weapons. We have a profitable
task ahead. He'll soon perceive
that those whom he has just proved
to be nothing are something indeed."   465

     Geta obeys his orders and
is the first to seize his arms.
They both make ready their weapons;
one is driven to avenge his bed's wrong;
the other prepares to deny with his sword
that he is nothing. Birria prefers
to dissemble. "By Hercules,"
he says, "I knew it. When I sought the ships,

the adulterer was already inside.   470
Therefore I was sent on my way;
Birria, they can't deceive you!
Madness drives these fools to ruin;
let them wage their own wars.
No one is ever safe in a battle;
if I have any say in the matter,
Birria will never fall before Mars."

    The lord gives the battle cry;
he urges them on, crying loudly,   475
"Seize your weapons; go on ahead!"

    "My burden slows me down," Birria
says. "I'll follow on after you two."

[AMPHITRYON] "Better throw it aside so we can catch
the adulterer and cut him down."

[BIRRIA] "Throw it aside? It's wrong to add
loss to loss. We aren't their equals;
perhaps there are many of them inside.
An adulterer won't be caught without   480
great force; fornicators
go heavily armed. I'll follow you,
go on ahead. The sword is a weapon
for hand-to-hand fighting. Standing apart,
I shall give aid from a distance,
hurling rocks from my sling.
Unexpected wounds often do the most harm."

    Amphitryon and Geta brandish their weapons   485
and go on their way, uttering many a threat;
both invoke Jupiter's aid in their fight
against Jupiter. Birria mocks them:
"Whence comes this audacity?" he asks;
"what madness is this? If the adulterer
only knew them. You are men
ready to turn tail. Had the Greeks
sent men like you into battle,   490

46

Troy would now still exist.
Birria, if you're clever, you will be
the first to flee, the last to attack.
Nothing is safer than timorous flight."

By now Jupiter's ardor burned
a little more coolly; the kisses the lovers
exchanged were rather less passionate.

[JUPITER] "Duty calls me. I left my ships   495
on the shore lying unguarded.
Geta, make ready." He finished his speech.
Archas appears. Heaven rejoices
in Jove's return. The earth smiles less,
perceiving that the gods have departed.

Alcmena was unadorned; she had removed
all her finery, like one who has
already given great pleasure.   500
Every door stands open. Amphitryon
appears, fully armed. The woman is afraid
at the sight of his weapons; the frightened
wife starts at the sight of her husband.
"What need for a sword? Take kisses, not arms,"
she says. "This is not the way you used
to approach me." Her mild words charm him;
still fully armed, he embraces her.   505
His sword slips from his hand; his wrath
cools. Geta steals up, amazed
to see the door now unbolted.
He tries to discover the adulterer
although fearful lest he should succeed.
Finding no trace of a lover, Geta
grows bolder. He goes out,
and having nothing to fear, gives vent   510
to terrible threats: "Amphitryon,
where has that adulterer gone to?
You've kissed long enough; where's her lover?
Soon he will fall, cut down by my sword.
And let Alcmena tell us why

47

all the doors were barred to Geta."

     She laughs and answers him, "You were
guarding the gates. You shut them,   515
you opened them up. And then, at your pleasure,
you shut them again. And I was embracing
Amphitryon in my bedroom."

     Her words distress Amphitryon.
The kissing is broken off. Harsh words
disturb their peace. He attacks those cheeks   520
which he'd just been caressing. "Woe is me,"
he cries. "We came straight up the road.
By god, there was an adulterer here!"

     "No, there was not," she replies.
"Indeed, I saw you, or I think that I saw —
often my mind is beguiled by such dreams."

     "These are some dreams," adds Birria   525
aside. "Geta is mad, made more a fool
than before by his erudition.
Away with all these insane disputations.
I'm on my way to the kitchen.
Let Amphitryon be happy, let Geta be a man."

     Amphitryon rejoices in his wife;
Birria rejoices in his gleaming kitchen,
and Geta, he's glad to be a man.   530
Each one of them is contented.

Notes to *Geta*

1. Text taken from the edition of Bertini, 1980.

2. The names of the slaves are all taken from Terence; Birria is a character in the *Andria*.

3. I have preserved the tenses of the original here. In general, Vitalis used the present tense to introduce a speech, and a past tense for concluding remarks. I suspect that this practice may be an indication of a mimed performance.

4. As Bate notes in his edition, there were various qualities of bread available in the Middle Ages.

5. The names come from Terence's comedies.

6. I preserve the Latin tenses here.

7. This line sounds like an internal stage direction.

8. I retain the original tenses here.

AULULARIA[1]
(The Pot of Gold)

By Vitalis of Blois

ARGUMENT

Querulus' father committed his gold to a fragile pot,
putting his trust in a funerary epitaph.
Then he went abroad; on his deathbed
he entrusted his secret to a slave
who thought to deceive Querulus on his return.
He became a magician to exorcize Querulus' house   5
and got in. He stole the pot, but deceived by the inscription,
he thought that it contained only bones.
He returned it, tossing it into the shrine, and it broke;
out poured the gold. Querulus was on the spot,
and he gathered up the scattered coins.
Lying, the slave said that he'd returned it willingly
and found credibility in deceit; his deeds were approved.   10

PROLOGUE

Whoever rereads Plautus will perhaps be amazed
to find the characters in my work bearing new names.
There's a very good reason. Poetry needs domesticated words.
The meter shrinks from names longer than normal.[2]
Therefore I've changed or chopped short the names   15
for the sake of the meter; nonetheless, the plot is the same.
Should someone charge that my comedy talks about fate
and the stars, and sings too lofty a strain —
should someone say that my humble pen has rebelled
and has foolishly aspired to grandeur —   20
why that's Plautus' fault, not mine.
I am free from all blame; I'm only following Plautus,
and the subject demands great things for itself.[3]
This comedy — mine or Plautus' — gets its name from a pot,
but that which was Plautus' is now mine.
I have curtailed Plautus, and he is enriched by the loss;   25

Vitalis' writings earn applause for Plautus.
First the *Amphitryon*,[4] and now the *Aulularia*,
long oppressed by age, rejoice in Vitalis' help.

The House of Querulus

Angered by fate, Querulus blames the authors of his
ill-omened name, and grieves that the gods exist.   30
"What," he says, "did the gods intend when,
at the beginning of time, they apportioned
unformed globs out into shapes?
No doubt so a harsh, bitter destiny might singe
those exposed to fate, and more easily too.
It would have been better if everything slept in the bosom   35
of nature, and lay buried in a barren mother.
Now there's toil everlasting, hardship unending,
which undoes everything so that everyone survives
but wishes he hadn't. If only it were so for all,
then fate would be tolerable; if evil fate
were the same for everyone, then I'd be content.   40
Hardship hurts less when it's shared around.
But why do all the gods have it in for me?
I was born for continual complaining, and am called
Querulus because my life's one long complaint.[5]
I complain about my fate and see a portent in my name.   45
Just hear my name and you'll know my lot.
I am wretched; I take my name from my fate.
Hardship proves the omen of a new name.
My name attracts my fate. I'm led by my lot.
Or should I consider my name the cause of my fate?   50
No. I'd have been unhappy had Julius been my name.
If I changed my name, I'd still have tough luck.
But I still marvel that whenever I stick my nose out of doors,
hark, my name can be heard on everyone's lips.
The mob hisses at Querulus, and follows me about,   55
and I can't go anywhere without attracting a crowd.
People look at me askance on account of my name.
What evils little by little come into existence,
all on account of the names which fathers   60

51

bestow on their sons! How much better it would be
if at adolescence one could pick any name one liked!
I who am now called Querulus could have been heir
to a grand and dignified name. I could be
Plato, Socrates, or even Pythagoras. No,
I hate Pythagoras because he shunned eating meat   65
and thought that a pig was his kin. [6]
How many mistakes does the mind of man teach us
in its desire to discover the truth; as for
the truth, *its* desire is to stay well hidden.
Jupiter keeps men's hearts in suspense by such means,
lest men find some way to be happy.   70
Daring to pry into the secrets of nature,
Plato discovered and taught that there's only one god.
Whence, weaving together the web of necessary order
with an ambiguous fate, he taught that the gods do not exist.
Thus he explains fate by fate, so that chance rules   75
everything, although there's necessary order in it.
And again he explains fate by fate in such a way
that chance itself governs our course by its necessary law. [7]
Ergo: Querulus is necessarily wretched,
nor can he fail to be wretched, if we are
to believe in this philosophical school.   80
I hate Plato's dreams woven of ambiguities,
since he strove to sing things I can't understand.
This alone pleases me: he says there's no swarm of gods.
His doctrine, even if wrong, will be useful.
Man lives for the gods; now nobody works for himself;   85
should you be rich and worship all the gods —
you'll soon be a pauper. Man's foolish piety
rejoices to serve gods which he has created,
and he alone makes the gods exist.
He fears his own handiwork and obeys its orders —
poor wretch, he doesn't know how to live free.   90
In this house two altars used to be dedicated to the Lar,
and we made Fortune into our household Lar. [8]
From that time on Fortune has been angry with us
and with the god himself. She won't do a thing
for wretched little gods. Nevertheless,
first thing every morning we pray, 'Grant, holy Lar.'   95

I don't know what he can give me since he's got nothing himself.
The Lar is granted the guardianship of the hearth,
but he's a bad guardian for me; if I don't take
good care of him, he'll not be safe. He who needs a protector
is himself not very good at protecting.[9]
If the Lar is my god, what need has he of me?   100
If men had any sense, the whole pack of gods could go begging;
as it is, the proper order's reversed, and it's man
who nourishes the gods. At least man ought to be
the god of the gods: Querulus' god
is whichever one feeds him well.
Lar, go seek another hearth for yourself! Religion   105
has never given me a thing, nor will it do so.
My father, always a spendthrift, built altars for the gods,
and tombs too, and took care for grandfather's bones.
That was an ill omen; the house is cursed as a tomb;
the house has omens of a funereal fate.   110
What good did the gods do those who cherished them?
Listen: that man, a sincere devotee of the gods,
died an exile! If you want to consider
any man happy, you must look to his end.
No one's to be accounted happy before he's dead.[10]
A voracious slave oppresses Querulus in his home,   115
and abroad the jealous are after him:
thus an evil lot assails me on every side.
How wicked of envious fate to unite Pantolabus and Querulus;
I am querulous on his account; it's his deeds
I lament. Having dined well, he picks a quarrel
with me on the grounds that he is barefoot,   120
as though I were born to take care of him
rather than myself. The empty belly
falls peacefully to sleep on any old pile of straw.
Hunger grows with eating; food itself makes one hungry.
I've consulted physicians; they call it 'boulimy,'
that is, an appetite just like a dog's.
The doctors have made this consumer voracious;   125
their cures have increased his continual hunger.
Such is medicine's success: if you feel a bit poorly,
just go to the doctor — soon you'll be sick.
And this is the final step in degradation:

without stealing, there's no way to get rich." 130

Querulus and the Lar

Thus Querulus — angry at himself, at his slave,
at the very gods — was everyone's enemy.
The Lar was at hand, about to bring aid,
but he who is prepared to alleviate a sad fate
only makes it worse. He who condemns ill luck
gives pleasure; he who helps out is unwelcome. 135
Brave words only irritate troubled minds.
"Long life to Querulus," he says.

"Long life?"
Querulus replied. "With my wretched luck, you can't give me
anything worse; my evil fate is worse if prolonged;
if brief, at least it has some little good. 140
Death enriches the poor, and the fates subside with fatality.
Give long life to the unfortunate — his ill fortune increases."
"Not so," says the Lar. "If you think yourself
unfortunate, you can't be unfortunate;
chance doesn't make you unlucky, only opinion. 145
If you are stalwart in mind, chance will be disarmed."

[QUERULUS] "You are teaching men to go mad. What monsters
will you see if the wretch ignores his wretchedness!
The one who's unhappy is wrong if he thinks he's not,
nor will anyone be happy just because he ignores his fate." 150

[LAR] "Don't interrupt my words with your continual replies.[11]
Silence is better; learn to speak silently."

[QUERULUS] "I beg you, don't talk so much. Just do something!
Show me in deeds what you teach in words.
The gods have done a lot of talking but precious
little giving; how easy it is to talk, 155
but it is the doing that counts."

[LAR] "Things are constrained and controlled by a succession

of preordained events. Things transpire in accord
with Jove's command. There is an order to order.
Where the divine mind wishes, it stops,
and where it is unfettered, it has
the means to make progress. The thoughtful order   160
of the mind explicates the implicit; it wanders
not by a random error; it is mobile, but not without law.
Thus it knots up the unknotted, and thus the divine order
binds all up, blessing everything because there is no place
for the unfortunate."

[QUERULUS]   "I never thought that my Lar   165
was a Platonist. Blessed Plato, he taught the gods.
If a thing keeps its place, he burns with delight,
but what will he feel if it finds a miserable place?"

[LAR] "The more I cure you, the more gravely you become ill,
and my medication only makes you sicker.   170
Through the doctor's skilled hands, pain increases
in order to decrease; the more it is pressed hard,
the less the wound is injured. Your fate is changing
in order that you may be changed along with it.
So that you may please yourself, your fortune is now displeasing."

[QUERULUS] "The gods deceive poor wretches with fraudulent   175
promises, neither true nor worthy of belief.
So they may get their gifts they always command men to hope,
until an affair which has turned out badly demonstrates
the vanity of hope. The cheerful promiser is slow
to make good, though bold in promising
and utterly lacking in credibility."   180

     The Lar had left the house, abandoning complaining Querulus
to his complaints so that he'd stop his complaining.[12]
His grief decreases as far as groans go, but pent up,
it overflows. Enclosed fire burns the hottest.[13]

Euclio, Sardana

Querulus' father was overwhelmed by much traveling;   185
Lachesis took his fate in her hand.
Old age, together with toil, were summoning death,
and approaching death orders him to entrust all
to his slave. The slave is close at hand,
hovering about his old master and caressing him,
and he captivates him in with sedulous attention —   190
not because of any love for his master but to cheat him
and worm out his secret. This slave doesn't love well.
He sits beside the old man who says, "You know,
my dear Sardana, that I have been not a master
but a father to you; unlike the common run of masters,
I didn't want to abuse my power over you,   195
nor did I treat you like a slave.
And what's my reward for that? You have been
most devoted to me, and your trustworthiness is true,
for I have bought it many a time. Listen carefully:
reliability, devotion, and secrecy are what I need.
I'll tell you everything. In my house,   200
in the corner where stands the altar of the Lar,
a trusty pot holds a thousand talents of mine.
Fate has condemned me to fathering an unworthy heir,
nor could any son be worse than he is.
Indeed, I'd have no fear if my son were extravagant,   205
but I do fear his rash manner of spending.
Oh, would that he knew how to be either stingy
or extravagant! Both are evils, yet both can do
some good. Both are faults yet useful as well.
Open-handedness increases friendships; tight-fistedness   210
increases one's wealth. But money given to fools
only makes trouble. Now poverty restrains him;
since he has no money, he has to be wise.
A pittance prevents him from being satisfied;
he's afraid to make a mistake. But he'll like
the wealth which will minister to his folly.
Money entrusted to the ground has escaped Querulus,   215
and the pot has been more loyal to me than my son.
We've been traveling away from home for seven years;

crippling old age is upon me.[14] Woe is me!
I marvel that such is the place of my death,
but I do not complain of our common condition.   220
This is nature's law, that things joined together be unjoined.
The god's ire allots to each the place of death.
It's sweet to die at home, to kiss one's dear children,
to apportion one's bequests, giving each his due.
To pass away amidst a wife's tears,[15] to be borne   225
to the pyre in a father's arms, as a mother bears the torch —
this is a proper funeral, these are the comforts for dying
(a poor consolation but better than nothing).
Sardana, an angry fate has left me only you,
and mother earth will receive me, with your assistance.   230
I am consumed by concern for my heir. May he live
honorably, for my life continues in him.
Since he's not very clever, I must be the more concerned for him.
But I am worried; love commands me to act like a father.
Perhaps his teacher, and experience and maturity, and,   235
most important of all, hunger (which teaches men
deceit) have compelled him to grow wise.
And even if he still is a fool, it's better
that my property be lost by him than lie buried
forever in the ground, which is thereby enriched.
The affair needs someone to reveal it; my son will inherit
one thousand talents when you tell him all,   240
and take ten talents for yourself as a reward.
I free you of the yoke of servitude; depart a free man.
You who just now were Sardana will be called Paul.
Off you go, a free man, and good luck go with you,
and be as concerned for me as I am for you."

     In tears he stopped speaking, and Sardana   245
pretended to sob lovingly. They both weep,
but one is full of sorrow, the other of joy.
A funeral urn received the old man. The service, however,
was cut short; the servant took off before its conclusion.
How badly a slave loves! If fear is removed, loving
ceases. He doesn't love in order to fear   250
but he fears in order to love.[16]

Emboldened with his master's money, Sardana
conceives great plans. Now he's free.
Now he's Sardana no longer but his own man.
How wrong it is when riches are put to a slave's use!
A rich slave is worse than an serpent.
As he wends his way home, and has time and opportunity,   255
he makes his own plans in this fashion:
"Sardana, happy in recent good luck, dare to be
even happier. A lucky turn has renewed your hopes;
let's see about making them even better.
Poverty prevents one from aspiring high, but the old man's
goods are available; I shall enjoy his riches!   260
He lies in the ground. He lies there, and there let him lie.
The gods certainly never dispense justice better
than when they cause a miser to go without.
He lived for me alone. Fate has arranged things very nicely.
The one who is his own enemy betrays himself.
Whoever you are, rejoice now lest your heir rejoice   265
when you die. Spend! Otherwise someone else will have
all that wealth you've acquired. Querulus
lives like a beggar in a house full of riches,
and guards the gold, but not for himself.
He lives impoverished — rich, but not for himself.
When his father could have been loving, he wasn't,
and now calls himself loving when he can't be so.   270
Having shared his wealth as he liked, the old man bade me
inherit a mere fraction of those one thousand talents.
That's not a fair share, but I'm not Sardana
if I don't cheat Querulus and steal all thousand talents.
The consecrated whole, which the father feared to violate,   275
will not be divided; it's sin to break something
sacred. Broken faith, however, is useful.
Jupiter is fair only to the unjust, and he dies
who fears the gods. The error of a false name
will deceive Querulus. I shall no longer be called   280
Sardana but Paul. I shall be Paul, Paul,
the heir of the Roman consul. Under the name of Paul
Sardana will become famous. Well-known things are cheap.
That which isn't well known is desired. Act as if
you are unfamiliar, and you'll find yourself cherished."

Sardana summons his friends Gnatho and Clinia

The seventh day brings the servant home; one who is eager   285
doesn't know laziness. High expectations make all possible.
At night the home of an unknown host receives him.
Sardana takes care not to be seen; he takes pains
to be different and skillfully alters his appearance.
His features and the color of his lips obey his orders;   290
his hair, long well-cared for, he lets hang loose,
and it covers his neck and brushes his shoulders.
His shoulders slope downwards, and he holds his neck stiff,
raising high his head. He puffs his chest out   295
farther than usual, and his right hand gleams
under the weight of a ring of fake gold.
Luxuriating in a rich new cloak (he bought it
by robbing his master's corpse), he bids
his limbs to be luxurious. Sardana himself
now isn't sure that he's Sardana, and perhaps he'd convince
even himself if he put his mind to it.   300
He prefers the Roman race and tongue to the Greek,
and from time to time introduces foreign words;
he audaciously coins phrases not known to man
or to god — that way he acquires greater credibility.
He summons Gnatho and Clinia, friends in deceit,   305
through whom he arranges the trick he is cooking up.

"I have chosen you," he says, "whom experience has proven
my friends, so your help may lessen my worry.
I shall reveal my scheme and my *modus operandi*;
if there's a better one, let me benefit from your guile.   310
Querulus' father, defeated by death, told me his last wishes:
'In my house,' he said, 'one thousand talents are hidden.
One-hundredth of that sum shall be your share.
The rest is all for Querulus.' But I'd rather die,
I'd rather that anyone else should have it,   315
than have Querulus enriched with *my* help.
Fortune invites us to get rich. Let's go! The road
to easy fortune lies open before us. Look how great

59

are the honor and glory of wealth. Where there's plenty
of money, nobody asks where it came from.   320
Gold of devious provenience fetches just as good a price,
nor does that legally acquired gleam any more brightly.
Querulus exhausts fortune with his complaints and his gripes,
and he never stops grumbling about his lot.
Whoever can't endure bad luck only makes it worse.   325
If you complain of misfortune, it only grows harder.
    "Pretend that I'm the sort that Fortune hates
to hear making threats, and that I'm an adept in the
magical arts, able to alter an evil destiny,
to command the stars, to harm the gods with my spells.   330
Querulus is gullible. Under the guise of being
the source of bad luck, that pot will leave
the house, carried off by your hands.
But take care, for deceit, unless deceitfully concealed,
is no good at all. Lacking artifice, art perishes.
One of you two approach from where the stormy waves batter   335
Pallas' citadel; the other come from the opposite way.
One of you stop before the house of Querulus,
so that the other may approach at a run,
announcing that a magician has come; the other will hear it.
Do all of this so artfully that no artifice is suspected.   340
An affair lacks credibility if it appears to be
a put-up job. What's said impromptu, that seems the truth."

Gnatho: "You've said enough," he said, "and nothing more
is needed to get Gnatho busy thinking. I understand,
and, what is better, my professional pride is involved.   345
It only remains that the task be worthy of my skill.
Sardana, may the gods grant that Gnatho be worthy
to participate in your profitable scheme.
When I entice Querulus out of his house, be sure
to appear to be just what we are pretending.   350
Let your appearance reflect your condition.
Let your expression, so skilled at deception, play the role
you have chosen. Let your character be that
of a magician, your tongue that of a Roman,
your face that of a powerful man, your speech that of
a philosopher, your occupation that of a scholar.

60

Let the deceitful page of a mathematical table furnish you 355
with numbers, and keep books always open before you.
It detracts from credibility when fictions fail to agree.
Truth does not matter as much as the semblance of truth."

With Gnatho's aid, Sardana is raised up on a
lofty throne and hidden in the house's secret recesses. 360
Gnatho devises and directs the charade: "This is how
you should speak — to yourself, to Querulus, to me,
to all others. Take care to speak only a little;
those who babble are not taken seriously.
From time to time give a sideways glance at your books 365
so that he thinks you are reciting from them.
Writing will lend faith to your words; books confirm the truth.
What you do without their testimony will not be convincing.
You, my dear Clinia, take the road by the sea,
below the city walls and the Acropolis, while I 370
shall take this shorter route over here.
I shall be talking to myself; my words will be of wonders.
You are to come up and ask what amazes me so.
I'll refuse to tell, and you will entreat me.
I'll pretend, and you will push for an answer.
I'll get angry, and you will insist all the more. 375
I'll swear oaths and threaten, and you will swear
even greater oaths and add still greater threats.
It will appear to be a quarrel; Querulus loves a good fight.
He'll stand stock still at his door, eager to hear
every word. You will insist still more vehemently;
then, as if conquered by a friend's entreaties, I'll want
assurances that my secret is safe with you. 380
Don't hesitate to swear by the gods. This is the means,
this is the way that Querulus will be taken in."

Gnatho, Clinia, Querulus

His words are pleasing. Clinia takes a roundabout
route while Gnatho heads straight for Querulus' house.
He composes his features to mimic a false amazement 385
and speaks words which are those of one thunderstruck.
Now he raises his voice as if he wished to be heard,

61

and yet both wished and feared, for now he speaks softly:
"Nature does not treat men with equality or fairness,"
he said. "This one she oppresses, that other she blesses.   390
Nature zealously endows one with every good,
with others she's less energetic. She doesn't take
an equal concern for all of mankind,
and some she makes excel in virtue, others not.
Oh happy the kingdom before whom former glory gives way.   395
Rome, now blessed in real men, enjoys mastery of the world.
How happy powerful Rome, how pitiable poor Greece!
The land of Romulus possesses men who are veritable demigods;
one can really believe that the Latian race is descended
from the gods, and that the gods have shown themselves
partial to their own people. Why then do we fear   400
Aristotle, why fear old Plato? The whole of Greece
does not possess a single man the equal of this one.
He sings of the future as accurately as of past or present,
and he knows Jove's wishes better than Jove does himself.
No longer will Jupiter think up any surprises for him.   405
He has proven himself a true descendant of Aeneas."

    Querulus is glued to his half-closed door,
but fearing lest Gnatho stop talking, he shuts it again,
and says, "What can it mean when Gnatho, who never has
a good word for anyone, praises someone so highly?   410
I can scarcely believe that this enemy of all mankind
could ever speak a word other than an insult.
How has he chastened his tongue and lips,
usually so expert in inventing novel slanders for all?
He's unlearned bad habits, or else been conquered   415
by a friend's gift, or (which I would vastly prefer)
been converted by a club and threats for its use.
Whoever gives to rascals is just asking for trouble;
oppress them, and they will sing your praises.
Gifts encourage them; whips tame their spirits.
Whatever he commends, I'll find commendable:
praise from an enemy is more likely to be true."   420

    Clinia, having taken his shortcut, arrives opportunely
for Gnatho, and lends his assistance to the ruse.

"Tell me, Gnatho," he says, "whose praises you're singing,
and why are you lauding a Roman name to the stars?
Have the Roman youth done something amazing   425
which has earned them the reward of perpetual fame?"

    "Indeed," replied Gnatho, "I'm all wrapped up in this affair,
and it has put all other concerns right out of my mind.
I don't rejoice at Rome's misfortune, nor does her good luck
do me any harm; her losses don't distress me,
nor does her prosperity cause me joy. I've got a secret,
and things shared between two can't be called 'secret.'"

    Clinia insists: "Tell me, my dear fellow, tell me, I beg,"
he says. "Reveal your secret, if it's a profitable one.
You must share your problems with me, and don't let   430
your worry spoil our relationship — we two whom love
unites as one. No fortune blesses a man unless another know it,
and a happiness that's concealed bears no joy.
If there's call for a herald, I'll outdo trumpets and horns;
if it's silence you need, I'm better than a stone.   435
I shall be whatever you command."

                        Gnatho responds,
"No one is ever sufficiently true, even to himself;
more often than not one fails in reliability.
Often one forgets and says things which ought to be kept quiet,
and one's tongue is one's own betrayer.
Things wrongfully confided become common knowledge;   440
if the one keeps quiet, the other lets his tongue
wag freely. If this were a matter of little or no
significance, perhaps I would already have told you,
but its very importance bids me keep silent.
It's a matter for one alone. It is to my advantage   445
and I am not my own enemy. That which falls into pieces
becomes less and less useful; the greater the number
concerned, the less is the share of each one."

    "Dear friend," says Clinia, "an even greater desire to be
partner to your discovery steals over me."

Gnatho dissembles, pretending to seek to escape.   450
The one entreats, and the other refuses;
the one tries to leave, the other holds fast:
[GNATHO] "Either let go," he says, "or else you'll experience
Gnatho's strength on your head and your shoulders."

"Clinia's might is no less," the other replied.
"The one's who's experienced it only once fears him.   455
But because I'm getting nowhere with prayers, nor am I one
to compel, go away, but...."

                    "Oh, you've conquered me
with your prayers," Gnatho responds. "I've a marvelous nature.
Should you have chosen force, you wouldn't have heard a word,
but try entreaties and I'm all compliance.
Neither Herculean labor nor the arms of Caesar   460
can sway the one whom gentle entreaties can soften.
I'll tell you the matter with which Fortune has blessed me,
but I'd like to be sure my secret is safe with you."
The other swears by the god of heaven and son of Coronis, [17]
the greatest of all the divinities in Greece.   465

Querulus pays close attention, applying his ear to the door.
His whole attention is in listening lest he miss a word.
"It's a serious matter," he said, "for he was prepared
to blurt out the whole thing, even against his will.
The other had scarcely finished his entreaties."

"Now, Clinia," Gnatho replied, "hear what fortune,   470
kinder than any deity, has granted me to know.
But come over here, lest someone be lurking at the door
who could furtively overhear the whole story."
He had already seen Querulus hiding there.
That man withdrew from the door and listens   475
now from this side of the house, now from that. [18]

"You know," Gnatho says, "how hard poverty oppresses me,
how hard and for how long. But it's come to an end.
The end of hardship is at hand. Your Gnatho could not
be poor any more, even if he should want to be.

64

A new fate has brought to this city a man or a god,   480
I don't know which. He appears to be a man in body
but in mind he's a god. Nature wanted this man
to know so much that, although a human,
he rivals the gods of heaven in wisdom.
Why, he knows Jupiter's mind better than Jupiter does,
and whatever the gods are thinking and what new fates   485
are in store. Heaven serves his will.
The rigid order of destiny does his bidding
and goes where he compels. He checks Jupiter's purpose
and orders Jupiter to do what *he* wants, willing or not.
Thus he plays Jupiter to Jupiter. He's not a magician
but ought to be considered magic incarnate.   490
Art is nothing to him for he has created art itself.
Nor does he know only what the morrow will bring,
or what the present hour portends,
but what a distant time will reveal, what Jupiter
intends in one thousand years — all this *he* controls.   495
But why should I delay you with further details?
Were ours a religious age, Gnatho would think him a god.
By potent charms of strange power he exorcizes
evil from any house whatsoever, and
once the evil has fled, it will not dare to return.   500
The house will be prosperous for eternity.
I've hurried here because there's such strength in his power
that I hope to buy his aid, whatever the price.
The force of friendship grows in strength with gifts;
the tongue encourages giving; gifts win hearts."   505

        "I want to know his reason for coming, his country,
and his name," Clinia says.

                Gnatho answers each query:
"His name is Paul, and being descended from the consul
Paul, he ennobles an already noble race.
Rome, seat of the gods, home of mighty kings,   510
Rome, generous with her law, has sent him
so that he may instruct the Greeks, and so that Greece
may be indebted to Romans for arts, as she is for generals."

65

"I'm all afire," replies Clinia, "with desire to see him.
Good luck has granted us the presence of the Roman magician.[19]   515
If ever I have done you a favor, or can do one in the future,
let me lay eyes on this prodigy, if only once."

Gnatho responds: "I won't begrudge you a thing,
but I don't want you to spread abroad the good news
of the happy time which a new chance is going to give us,
when the number of our retinue and the purple and jewels   520
of our garb will make us revered, will make us new men.
We'll be the ones to laugh, to be the object
of the admiration of the humble folk,
for if anyone's wealth increases, his status grows with it."

Clinia urges haste; Gnatho concedes; they depart.
"Fortune," stammers Querulus, "this is for me!"   525
He leaps out, but his rush lands him on his head;
he catches his foot and falls flat on his face.
Laughing, Gnatho says to Clinia, "We have here an omen.
The booty I sought has fallen right into my snare."

"Gnatho, stop," calls Querulus. "Dear Gnatho, wait!"   530
They pretend to flee. He equals their speed and seizing
Gnatho with his right hand, Clinia with his left,
he entreats them with redoubled prayers:
"Dear friends, don't begrudge that I share with you,
me to whom my cleverness has revealed all."   535

Gnatho turns upon Clinia with a terrible scowl:
"I told you this would happen, you scoundrel!
Woe is me, poor Gnatho, for even when Fortune works hard
on his behalf and wants Gnatho to have good luck,
she is unable to do so. Poor wretch, I hamper
my good luck; I'm my own worst enemy; my fatal fondness   540
for Clinia has compassed my downfall!"
Clinia replies: "Who could have anticipated this loss?
A third companion won't do us any harm."

[GNATHO] "Won't do us any harm! Oh, it's a crime!
May the wrath of the gods fall upon your head!

Such reasoning could find us a fourth partner as well.   545
No doubt that Roman will freely pour forth miracles upon the mob,
things which I could barely convince him to reveal to me
for prayers and for payment!"

       "But every good,"
said Querulus, "will shine the more brilliantly
the more widespread is its enjoyment."

[GNATHO] "A plague on you! Go away!"

      Born to speak in proverbs   550
Querulus replied, "Ambiguous words engender curses."

Clinia checked Gnatho's bitter tirade: "Why,"
he said, "do you treat him as if he'd committed some crime?
He's one of us. If he's unhappy, spare him for my sake.
Fortune has been known to change her course overnight.   555
He chanced to overhear our conversation; let him profit from it.
Perhaps he will prove to be a useful companion.
No one is ashamed to be master to a crowd:
the more who attend, the more important one seems to be."

   Gnatho, Clinia, Sardana, Querulus

When Gnatho calmed down, he sought out the house   560
where Sardana was staying, and Querulus went with them —
their prey and their companion. Gnatho saluted
Sardana as he reclined on a lofty throne:
"Hail Paul," he said, "to you all honor from Jove."

Sardana mingles an unfamiliar language with a known one,
and uses ambiguous words as if he spoke with two tongues.[20]   565
In awe of his majesty they sat at a distance,
and fear of his power keeps them in silence.
"Young man," said Sardana, "now I shall reveal your fate
and shall prove myself most generous with my art.
So that you may know yourself better, I tell you   570
that your name is Querulus, your lot is an unjust one,

67

hunger dwells in your home, and you lack a father.
You have a gluttonous slave, Pantolabus, a useless monster,
who's hungry when full — he's hunger personified.
Twin altars to the Lar dominate your house
in front and in back; the whole house is dedicated
to the cult of the Lar. Therefore the Lar   575
possesses the whole house, and the house would be
prosperous, were the altar that of a real Lar.
But the Lar is nothing: fearful hearts have created the gods.
Your house will be lucky or unlucky in accord with my art.
In the interior of the house where the old altar   580
of the Lar stands, the ground is swollen. It's an ill-omened place —
an ill-omened place and detestable to the gods themselves,
one which even the Lar would hate, were he a real god.
Now I am casting your horoscope to learn what sign
has set for you or what the heavens portend in the stars.   585
Capricorn, rising, first directed his course
to where the line of the solstice makes Cancer set.
There was the king of the east whom we call Saturn.[21]
Mars showed himself in the tail of Scorpio,
while the dazzling sun made Jupiter retrograde,   590
and Venus, pushed out by Libra, weakly lay low in the sky.
Thus heaven revealed its wrath at your birth,
and you, oh ill-fortuned wretch, have as your sign
the deadly Saturn. But I have the power to compel
the stars to alter their course and can change destiny
with my charms. All will be well, exorcized by my art."   595

        Querulus gapes dumbfounded, and thinks Sardana's utterance
divinely inspired. He says, "You know me better than I do.
But I beg you, Paul, glory of the Roman race,
by art make Querulus cease to be wretched."
Clinia implores him as well, and Gnatho bows low   600
in supplication; Querulus is insistent.

        "All right, you win," says Sardana. "You win,
and I shall make this the first miracle
which Roman Paul performs on Grecian soil,
so that my glory may spread rapidly through Greece
and Paul may enjoy celebrity for his ability   605

throughout the whole world. But you, Querulus,
and you Clinia, and you too, Gnatho, remember
the words which I now am going to recite to you.
Incantations lose force if the order is confused,
and a loss of faith diminishes the words' power.
A charm needs order and rejoices in trust.   610
This will be the form of religious observance for you:
let the right foot precede, and not touch the doorsill;
let Querulus do all he is ordered, and nothing he's not;
let Gnatho repeat the words which I have pronounced,
increasing thereby the sound of my incantation.   615
As for Pantolabus, let him either remain ignorant
or let him learn how to keep his mouth shut.
In such delicate matters, every detail is significant."

     He stood up, and Gnatho dared to touch with his hand
the pretended holy book (he'd been ordered to do so),
while Querulus walks on ahead, conveniently foolish,   620
and invites his enemies in under his roof.
The front door stands open. Sardana recites a prayer
to purify the threshold, adjures the gods, and makes
a special sign on the ground. He nods to Gnatho,
signaling him to order them all to stand still,   625
to keep their hands quiet and to close their mouths.
Together all four cast down their eyes and ready their bodies:
thus does a hypocrite assume the semblance of piety.
Having purified the threshold with a fake prayer,
Sardana cries aloud as he lifts up his right foot
to enter the house, "May good luck reign in this house!"   630
Gnatho follows him and intones in a loud voice,
"May good luck reign in this house!" "Be gone, hostile fate,"
adds Sardana, and Gnatho repeats, "Be gone, hostile fate."
Sardana spies to the right and then to the left,
above and below, to find the pot's hiding place.   635
He measures the space, and having determined the distance
from the altar's edge, he orders them to dig a big hole
lest the dirt from the surrounding excavation
retain any trace of the iniquitous fate it had held.
Gnatho's right hand smites the ground with a pick-axe,   640
and the earth groans aloud beneath Clinia's blows.

Sardana says, "Querulus, dear, have an empty chest
made ready; if it's full, dump everything out."

"But," replied Querulus, "they're all empty, unless
you consider what's filled with air to be full."   645

[SARDANA] "Nothing is empty: the surrounding atmosphere
by its very lightness suffers no void to exist.
Since air keeps nothing out, nothing keeps it out,
and it permeates every substance through hidden pores.
This element is incapable of being made dense
so no space contains more air or less;   650
it neither escapes when something is added,
nor does it increase if you take something out."

The business is urgent. The chest is at hand.
The job is completed. Lest Querulus observe,
he is made to turn his back. The pot goes into the chest.
"Bear it away," says Sardana, and Querulus is ready   655
to obey the order. Querulus carries it out,
and the waiting hands of Gnatho and Clinia receive it.
Sardana points out the way. They hasten down
the appointed road, while Sardana instructs
Querulus on what remains to be done, but briefly
lest delay hinder his plan. Therefore he says,
"Every evil and all ill luck have fled far away.   660
There will be nothing further for you to fear.
Nevertheless, I advise you to close all doors and windows,
blockade the doors and shove home the bolts.
If Phoebus' rays shine in through a crack, block it up
so that entrance is denied even to Phoebus.   665
Defend your home with weapons; if you hear any noise,
run there and shout, 'Be gone, hostile fate.'
This importunate creature, ill fate, will be in a hurry
to revisit those places which she knows so well.
Be sure to do this for a full five days in a row."

Sardana, Gnatho, Clinia

Querulus did as ordered. Sardana runs after Gnatho's path, 670
and they take a roundabout route and cover their tracks.
When they are far enough away in a spot whose shadows
give promise of safe concealment, they put down the chest.
They take the pot in their hands and discover the inscription
which fraudulently declares it a funerary urn. 675
They see the inscription and are amazed; seeing the writing,
they think they see nothing; utter amazement holds them fast.
They read what is written and wonder whether
they've read correctly; he who read is afraid
to read more. They fear their fears are true, 680
and have both too much and too little confidence.
Their hope forbids, their fear commands them to believe.
They stand stock still, their gaze fixed,
as if thunderstruck, as if they've lost their tongues.

"Sardana, what does the inscription mean when it refers
to bones?" asks Gnatho, and Sardana replies, 685
"I don't know. You read it; you know Greek better than I.
Read out the words of the inscription." Gnatho reads:

THIS URN CONTAINS THE BONES OF TRIPERICIUS, FATHER
OF TRIPERUS; THEY WERE BURIED WHEN ROME'S POWER
WAS RESPLENDENT IN THE DAYS OF JULIUS CAESAR.

"I've got it!" said Sardana. "Now I remember 690
the old man once telling me, 'This is my father's urn.'
But because it's usually only at the hour of death
that secrets are revealed, I believed instead his dying words.
Either it was all a trick, or we've taken the wrong urn,
or else pain and grief made his mind wander. 695
Woe is me! I was hoping for happy times.
Now I'm compelled to abandon hope; my trick has been
trumped by the old man's treachery. Woe is me.
How far I've traveled, and for what? To read about
a bunch of bones! My expectations with hope 700
shortened the distance and lessened my exertion.
But when hope is dead, the sweet becomes bitter."

Gnatho urges that whatever is hidden in the urn

71

be exposed to view, lest their error
lead them even further into error,
but Sardana steps between the urn and the hand
raised to smash it, and he says:
"What's the good of gazing on bones? 705
The inscription proves the urn is a funeral one,
and bones are not disturbed with impunity.
Ghosts get angry; the shade remembers
its urn's injuries and demands retribution.
I think it would be more useful, since hope is forbidden, 710
that lasting joys replace empty hope.
I pretended to Querulus that ill-luck wished
to return to his house, and lest she get in,
that credulous fool goes about armed.
The back wall of the house is missing a brick;
there we'll throw the pot back into the house. 715
Querulus will run up and get angry with this burial —
the heir will learn that the pot contains his ancestor's remains.
We've lost everything, but he's lost just as much.
It's nothing. 'Don't count your chickens,' they say.
We've lost only hope. We pursued foolish profit 720
and lost, but he who laughs last laughs best."

And so they redouble their error. Deceit itself
is deceived. Deceit becomes deception.
"So be it," says Clinia, and Gnatho agrees.
Therefore the pot is returned, and as it is thrust
through the crack it makes noise, and it breaks 725
into smithereens. The stolen gold is returned
into the possession of another, its rightful owner.

Pantolabus, Gnatho, Sardana, Querulus, [Clinia]

Pantolabus, to whose care had fallen the rear of the house
cries out, "Master, come quickly over here!
Look, you chest's been returned, and with interest. 730
The pot has brought you back the gold it took away.
The gods have done far more than one could expect.
Deceit has duped the thieves; your possessions are safe."

72

The gold's gathered up; it numbers one thousand talents.
A more secure strongbox takes over its guardianship.   735
Querulus' mind isn't up to rejoicing; his delight
falls short of reality. Thus Querulus rejoices
less than he ought, and fails himself, even in joy.

Meanwhile Sardana, seeking some sport for himself   740
by looking in through the crack, witnesses his own loss.
"Alas," he cried out, "the gold was hidden in that pot!
Alas, my deceit has be duped by my deception.
Oh lying inscription! Why did it call gold bones?
My trick has failed, tricked by a hypocritical   745
funeral inscription. Woe is me, woe is you, Clinia,
and a double, a triple woe is you, Gnatho!
Indeed, we'll not have a day without woe."

They were confused and dumbfounded; they grieve,
then grief turns into anger: the due punishment
turns upon the author of the deception —
Sardana finds those he'd hoped were his friends
have become his enemies; each takes to his heels   750
in opposite directions. But the fortunate
Querulus is at hand: "Who," he says, "quarrels here?
Does he not fear to disturb my threshold
with strife?" (Good luck has made him bold; his pride
has increased. Thus minds are renewed though new fate.)   755
He looks at Sardana, who having removed
his strange garb and discarded his magical apparatus,
appeared, in fact, to be none other than Sardana.

"I'm punished for having kept faith," said Sardana.
"It was on my advice that the gold was restored.

Querulus feigns ignorance, as if he knew nothing of gold: 760
"What riddles do you speak? What are you chattering about?
Are you my Sardana? Are you that Sardana, companion
and slave of my father, who aided him in his travels?"

"I am he," he said, "sent to you so that the pot,
which had been cast aside, might render you its talents

73

through my revelation. In the first place I showed that   765
I could deceive you: thus by fraud have I proven my faith."

Arbiter, Sardana, Querulus

An arbiter had arrived to settle their quarrel. To him
Sardana said, "You are here, O worthy arbiter,
to judge us, and in accord with your judgment   770
will our quarrel be settled. Pass judgment on my rights,
and allot me the just reward for my loyalty.
The old man was defeated by death: 'I have, dear Sardana,'
he said, 'at home entrusted one thousand talents to a pot.
You take ten; the remainder is for Querulus.
Try to determine whether or not he has yet learned   775
how to take care of himself. First steal the talents,
then return them: having once suffered loss
in general makes people more cautious.
We are wary of known perils, but rash with regard
to unknown. Experience teaches how to escape danger.'
I steal, I give back; I keep my faith   780
both to you and to the old man — to the old man
by stealing, to you by restoring what I've stolen.
My deceit was without guilt, the theft was a loyal one.
My piety is proven in theft, and faith in my piety."

The arbiter said, "Your fraudless fraud has done well
by Querulus. Your loyalty is worthy of trust."   785
Querulus thinks it's all true, and Sardana wins
his case. False faith brings profit, and
quarrels are at an end. The action is pleasing.

74

Notes to the *Aulularia*

1. Text from the edition of Bertini, 1976.

2. Sardana has replaced Mandrogerus and Gnatho Sardanapallus; Pantomalus has become Pantolabus. For discussion of the choice of names, see Bertini, 1974. For the relationship to the pseudo-Plautine *Querulus*, see the introduction.

3. Cf. the similar disclaimer in *Geta;* also Ovid, *Fasti* 3.474, *Metamorphoses* 8.230.

4. I.e., Vitalis' *Geta*.

5. In Latin *querulus* has the same meaning as its English cognate.

6. A reference to the Pythagorean doctrine of metempsychosis.

7. A parody of the language of the schools. Later on, in his pretentious attempts at learned language, Sardana frequently contradicts himself (see, e.g., 582-83).

8. There is a play here on *Lar*, the household god, and the word's metonymic use as "household" or "hearth."

9. These three lines involve an untranslatable series of alliterative puns on *tutela, tutor, tuear,* and *tutus*.

10. A reference to the famous dictum which goes back ultimately to Herodotus 1.32.

11. As Bertini notes, the absence of such phrases as "said Querulus," "said the Lar," points to genuine dialogue and supports the thesis in favor of some form of dramatic representation from these works. The action would not be confusing for an audience watching a mime.

12. This kind of word-play, with four words utilizing the same stem (*Querulum, querentem, questibus, queri*), sounds very awkward in English but is one of Vitalis' favorite effects.

13. Cf. the similar proverb in *Pamphilus* 22.

14. Bertini in his note *ad loc.* points to parallels for the phrase *tarda senectus* ("crippling" or "slow old age") in Horace, *Satires* 2.2.88 and Tibullus 2.2.19.

15. These lines are practically a *cento* of classical allusions; Bertini in his notes cites parallels from Ovid (*Fasti* 3.692, *Metamorphoses* 10.399, 13.583, *Tristia* 1.3), Horace (*Carmina* 3.2.13), Lucan (5.281), etc.

16. The proverb, "oderint dum metuant" (let them hate so long as they fear), goes back eventually to Accius' tragedy, *Atreus* (203-204, Ribbeck[2]; see Bertini's note *ad loc.).*

17. Cf. the mixed-up oaths of *Babio.* Rather than looking to Aesculapius, son of Apollo and Coronis, it seems easier to assume that Clinia has confused *Coronis* with *Cronus*, father of Zeus.

18. These lines, flat as far as a purely read version is concerned, sound like internal stage directions; the ensuing scene, with Querulus popping out from behind his house to overhear, would be quite funny if staged.

19. As Bertini remarks, a clear echo of Dido's plea to Aeneas, *Aeneid* 4.317-18.

20. A pun is here involved on bilingualism (i.e. knowing both Latin and Greek), and being deceitful.

21. Sardana uses slightly deformed versions of the Greek names of the planets; here "Saturn" is *Phenon* (= *Phaenon*, "shining"), while in 589 he employs *Piron* for *Pyroeis* (Mars), and in 590 *Feton* (= *Phaethon*), for Jupiter.

BABIO[1]

THE ARGUMENT[2]

So that the meaning of these verses may be apparent, I offer some explanation for my readers to show first what the subject of the representation is, and about whom, and how.

The author introduces five principal characters[3] who speak to one another so that they may appear to converse with those before them, and so that there may be no mistakes about who is speaking to whom, the names of the five characters are Babio, Petula, Fodius, Viola, Croceus. Babio was a priest,[4] Petula, his wife, Fodius the servant of Babio and Petula. Viola was a certain girl, the daughter of the priest's wife, and not Babio's own daughter but his stepdaughter, whom Babio loved and Fodius[5] too, unbeknownst to each other. Croceus was a knight,[6] the *seigneur* of the town in which the girl lived, and he was the lord of Babio the priest. This Croceus loved the girl and wanted to have her, and the priest was upset. Fodius was having an affair with the priest's wife, that is, with Petula, and his master, Babio, had no proof although he had his suspicions. But Babio was not concerned because he loved the daughter more than the mother, but stealthily, for he did not want to tell anyone and even bribed dogs[7] lest they tell (as if they could speak); nevertheless, he never had an affair with her. He did not dare to speak but loved her in secret, whence he said: "I'm tormented with grief," etc.

PART ONE

BABIO: I'm tormented by grief. Indoors, outdoors,
it's always the same. If I grieve any more
I shall not be able to bear it.
Why am I so unhappy? I won't tell.
But then again, it's dangerous to conceal grief —
concealed wounds go uncured, they say.
There's no one, though, to whom I can confess,   5
no one in whom I dare to confide.[8]

77

Babio

The crow is not white, nor is any pledge
of good faith to be trusted. I'm afraid
to disclose the matter. I'm afraid,
if I did, that I'd become the subject of gossip.
I'd rather be hit on the head with a three-
knotted club. So I'll tell myself
my own troubles. I'm the only one I can trust.

enter a dog

But who's that? I heard a voice, I see a man.   10
I should have been silent, held my tongue.
The prudent crane extended his neck to see,
or so I've been taught. But who is it?
I am deceived. Grief deceives the grieving.
I'll go closer. It's a dog! Listen to him bark!
Dearest Melampus,[9] be quiet.
Don't forget that little gift I gave you yesterday.   15
I'm Babio. Don't bark so much, dear Melampus.

exit the dog

The dog has gone; my grief remains.
It is indivisible,[10] lacking mobility.
It's Viola who makes me grieve (let no one overhear!).
You see, Croceus wants her, wants my dear heart,   20
but I'll not give her; she'll not be given.
Croceus seeks her and I shall refuse.
But, Babio, you know that a prince's entreaties
are but threats in disguise.
But to say "I will give her" will kill me —
I'll have taken my own life. But if I don't
give her, the gallows will be the end of me.
I'm a dead man; either fear or love is my murderer.[11]   25
Well, I'm not afraid. It's better to die for love.
But Babio, you're a rabbit, a coward,
if I know you at all. Should a tiny mouse
but cross your path, you'd lose your head.
I've done marvelous things nonetheless.
Once there were three of us; a shadow appeared.

78

We expected a wolf (it was only a tiny mouse); 30
we all panicked. The others took to their heels;
I followed, fearfully limping along behind,
but it was to my glory that, as we fled,
I fled the slowest.

But how can I bear
to part with my dear companion, Viola,
from whose lips, bees, you could gather your honey?
Stars are her eyes; her hair, Phoebus, it's just like yours. 35
She's Phyllis in her fingers, Thais in her feet.[12]
She has Helen's face, the trim waist of Corinna.[13]
Her smile rivals the noonday sun, her teeth rival ivory.
Seeing one so fair, blessed is the man who can touch her.
His days are fragrant with incense, his nights with balsam; 40
There's not a single flaw in her beauty, if only
her heart be true, if only she'll stay here with me,
if only she will refuse to go!
Viola and Croceus have nothing in common.
Their colors are different;[14] so may their hearts be, I pray.
I shall go and speak to her. I shall try 45
to make firm that delicate girl's resolution,
but to make solid such delicate fragility
will be, I fear, a far from trivial task.

[*to Viola*]

Flower of violets, Viola, splendor of flowers
inviolate, the picture of spring, the beauty of noonday,
gem of your family, the happy creation of your parent,
and, if the gods don't begrudge you the title, 50
practically a goddess yourself.
Dear Viola, more lovely than a violet,
more precious than riches, more beauteous than beauty,
and far more precious than the flower of crocus[15]
(which I curse); if you will but spurn
his enticements, I shall be safe.
Though I did not beget you, you're far dearer 55
to me than a child ever could be.
Though not my daughter, you are more than daughter to me.

Will you stay or depart? If you stay,
I can go on living; if you go, I can't.
You hold my life in your hands.
I grant you that Croceus is handsome,
and my shape, well, it's unshapely.
But he's no Paris, and I'm no companion to monsters.   60
Pepper has value; black wool is desired,
and snow, though it gleams, is a nuisance.
Be my mistress; I, my sex intact, will be your underling.[16]
Croceus wants to be king, Babio will be your slave.

VIOLA: What's Croceus to me? Let him chose   65
whomever he wants. Neither force nor entreaty
nor even profit will pledge him to me.
Should he feed me on gold,
cover me in Tyrian purple,
should he give me the world,
he would mean nothing to me!
The pole star will set, the ocean run dry,
before, dear Babio, Viola ceases to be yours.   70
[*Aside*] It would be life to escape you, death to remain.
If only *anyone* would carry me off; delay is torture.

[*exit Viola*]

BABIO: Now night has fled, now day dawns in my heart;
I was adrift on the ocean, now I've reached the shore safe.
You've given me everything! I'm rich as Croesus,   75
as free as Augustus, as potent — well almost — as Jove.[17]
I'm utterly happy, if you're as good as your word;
I'm blissfully happy, if your performance is as good.
You'll smother me with kisses, then start in again,
your lips' perfume scenting the air . . .   80
What's that noise in the house? My ears itch.
Someone will be talking about me.
Pray God he has only good things to say.

[*exit Babio*]

FODIUS: Now there are many plows working hard just for me.

80

Henceforth my affairs will go just as I'd like.
My enemy, Viola, is going away.   85
Now I will be able to enjoy Petula in safety.
With Viola gone I'll be free for deceit.
I detest that girl, always putting her nose
into my affairs. Now there'll be no one
to set traps for me. I'll go tell Petula.

[*to Petula*]

Your rival is going to marry Lord Croceus.
Work for that goal with all your might;   90
I'll work too. I was standing behind the door.
Viola was in the courtyard; she and Babio
were discussing the matter together.
She opposed him (from my hiding place I heard her):
"May God send me far away! I fear delay more than death."
Look, there's Babio inside. I'll go see what he's doing.   95
I hear noises in there; those noises have meaning.

[*Enter Babio; Babio to Fodius*]

BABIO: Look, here comes Lord Croceus. He wants
to marry Viola. He wants Viola.
He'll have to kill me first!
My faithful Fodius, hurry! Get this cow dung
out of here. Sweep the floor clean.
Put down fresh reeds. Pile more wood on the fire.   100
Scatter the straw around. Put a chair
over here, and a soft cushion on it.
Tell the cooks to get a move on
and to prepare a magnificent feast.
Kill a chicken — no, wait, that's too much.
Put half aside and serve the other to Croceus,   105
and, just as usual, beans and cabbage
for his companions. Here's a whole farthing;
go buy some bread, fish, wine.
We needn't serve quite so much, but do it anyway.
Make sure that Petula comes out from her chamber

81

to greet our guest, and make just as sure
that Viola stays hidden well out of sight,   110
locked up tight. I'll run out to meet him
and try to put on a cheerful face,
but who can really be cheerful
when guests such as these come to visit?

FODIUS: O Babio, Babio, more hateful than any owl,
into the dungheap with you and your farthing!
What a fine feast we're going to have,
cutting a scrawny chicken in two.   115
Cabbages and beans — this will be a fine marriage!
You'll always be just what you are —
thistles never have borne grapes.
When you turn generous, our ass
will be turned into a fine horse!

[*Enter Croceus and his companions*]

BABIO [*Aside*]: Look, I see Croceus and Entolus[18] before him,
and behind, Gluttonius Ventripotentous   120
together with Bavo,[19] that champion guzzler.
It's a legion. Oh poor Babio!
Entolus and Croceus, Gluttonius and Bavo!
Let me add it all up on my fingers
just to be sure that I'm right —
one, and two, and three, and four —
I can scarcely count that high.
[*Aloud*] My lord Croceus, farewell to you   125
and to your companions. [*Aside*] Alas, I said "farewell";
I do wish that had been right.
My lips expressed my true desire.
I'm not one of Satan's hypocrites.
Pray God I can correct myself and offer
the courteous greeting. [*Aloud*] Peace be to you and yours.
What happy chance brought you our way?
[*Aside*] That went pretty well; Babio's not a complete boob.   130
[*Aloud*] How sorry I am that you come here so rarely.
[*Aside*] How I wish you'd take a trip just now

right to the far side of the Alps!
[*Aloud*] Let us go in. Siddown. I spoke incorrectly.²⁰
I should have said, "Would you care to be seated."
I made a mistake. I wanted to use good grammar,
but my tongue's out of practice.
I do know logic though. Having thought over   135
the proposition most carefully, I am prepared
to prove that Socrates is Socrates
and that a man is a man.²¹
Someone once said incorrectly, "Dear master,
come here." But I taught him to say,
"Dear mister, wontcha come 'ere."
Let water be provided for them all
to wash their hands. Pour it out now.
Set the tables. My Lord, will you please   140
to sit down the first, and your people after.
Bring in the beans and cabbage —
that's the entree for your companions.
For Croceus we have the thigh of a chicken
and the wing too! When he's eaten his fill,
the others may have what's left over,
Entolus and his friends, Gluttonius and Bavo.
Entolus, when will you drink? Bavo's not drinking?   145
Drink up, Gluttonius. What poor drinkers you are!
[*Aside*] I'll ruin myself, talking this way.
[*Aloud*] My lord, eat. Why, what are you doing?
I pray you, please dunk your bread.
[*Aside*] May this be the last piece of bread
that you dunk. [*Aloud*] Take it away, he's had enough.
Be polite and give him some water. The doctor
wants everyone to bathe after eating.   150

CROCEUS: I repeat my request. I want Viola.
I won't be denied. Bid her enter. Tell her to come in.
Why is she hiding?

BABIO: She's sick.

CROCEUS: She has nothing to fear.
Let her come, let her come; we'll make peace and depart.

BABIO: Viola, although you're ill, if you feel up to it,
please come in here, just for a minute.
[*Aside*] Please don't come; be sicker than sick.   155
You won't come if a woman can keep her word.

[*enter Viola*]

FODIUS: Viola should marry Croceus; they both
have flowers' names, and like should be united
with like. Nothing is more harmonious.
Petula has no objections and neither do I. [22]

BABIO [*Aside*]: May no good come your way, vile wife, evil
  slave!   160
[*Aloud*] Viola, do you want Croceus?

VIOLA: If *you* wish it, I do.

BABIO: What's my wish? Choose the man *you* want,
that's what I wish. This smoke is getting in my eyes.
Away with it. [*Aside*] Viola, you're the one
who is making me cry.

CROCEUS: Get up. To horse. Put Viola on the mule.   165
Peace be with you, Babio, and good health, I pray.

BABIO: Oh how painful are peace and good health now
to Babio, sick at heart. I'm barely alive.
I rush toward death. How can you bear this, Petula?
Your sister [23] is carried away, and you just stand by?
Be an Amazon! Seize your weapons!   170
Fodius, run into the thick of the battle;
I'll be right behind you, whirling my sling.
Beat him up! I'll follow behind throwing stones. [24]
No, wait. There are only three of us.
Petula's just a weak woman, and Fodius,
he's barely more than a boy, and Babio,
why he's almost an old man. [25]

FODIUS: Babio's quarrels never do come to blows;   175

84

I've learned that his threats rarely break bones.
Why, if your enemies had been like him,
Troy, you would still be standing;
the Greeks would never have recaptured Helen.[26]

[*somewhat later*]

BABIO: Right now Croceus is violating Viola;
he's playing the game for two players.
Now he's touching her secret places.   180
Resist this dishonor, you slut!
You've suffered violence, Viola, and now,
I expect, you find that you like it.
      "And," that's a copula, a conjunction.[27]
Soon "And" will make you man AND wife.
That which I planted, he's carried off.
I planted the seed; he's reaped the harvest.
I cut down the brambles; another's caught the bird.
I'm still alive but I've lost my soul;   185
he took that when he took my Viola from me.
I marvel to find that a body can live[28]
deprived of its soul. I am Babio —
no, I'm not. I'm already dead.
But then who am I who is speaking?
Somehow I'm not the Babio I once was.
From nothing I have returned unto nothing.
I wish I really were nothing; I complain
because I am still something. I'd rather not be.   190
      A woman's heart is always the same — a woman's;
and every woman has not one heart but two.
Every woman has a double heart, double tongue,
and Viola's duplicity has taught me my speech.
Who would trust Viola now, but then, who   195
would have distrusted her either? Croceus
better not trust her, if he'll trust me!
      But just as the dawn disperses the shadows,
dispelling black night, so other women
have thought my Petula a prize.
She's not at all like Viola —

85

Viola is faithless but Petula faithful.
The one is night, the other day;   200
one is a bramble, the other a rose;
one is a wolf, the other a little lamb;
one is a treacherous serpent, the other a gentle dove.
One of the two is flighty and fickle,
but the other is constant and true.
Petula is every virtue, Viola every vice.
A wolf — no, a viper — bore her out in the thickets;
deep in hell's depths an Erinys nursed her.
Oh, how unlike are the two! One is immature,   205
the other mature, perhaps a wee bit worn
but nevertheless still fresh — both
a little more and a little less fair.
No, the child does not resemble her mother,
but then oil has dregs, wine has them too.
Wool breeds moths and water freezes to ice.
Petula's no Penelope but she comes pretty near.[29]
She is Chastity herself — no, nearly more chaste.   210
Petula's not petulant, she's not fickle,
not silly. Why, she's practically a man —
a woman with a man deep inside her.
Petula is Penelope in piety, a Sabine in modesty,
a Livia[30] in elegance, a Marcia in fidelity.
Babio, you should cultivate her once again,   215
repay the debt you owe her.
Devote yourself to her wholly;
be faithful henceforward only to her.

PART TWO

BABIO:[31] People are saying, Babio, that Fodius
has his way with Petula, that they're hard at work
on their knees, striving to increase the species.
If you remember the past, consider the present.
The facts prove that Fodius is not the Fodius   220
he once was. Once Fodius was poor,
his cheeks hollow, his feet bare, his hair dirty,

his body befouled with mud, his clothes
all hanging in rags. Suddenly he's been transformed.
His cheeks have filled out, he has shoes on his feet,
hair that's tidy, a clean body, nice clothes.
He struts elegantly, his shoulders thrown back,   225
his eyes looking boldly ahead.
His speech is haughty, his doings extravagant.
And where does all this luxury come from,
all these seven-course banquets? Where has he procured
all these things, and so cheaply too?
From you, Babio. It's not for your sake
that Petula's so thrifty. While she serves him,
the slave is the one who gets all of the gifts.   230
And while he is servicing her in his fashion,
it is Babio who is badly served!
A curse upon such distinguished service.
Viola was bad enough; Fodius is far worse.
I don't know which is the worse, they're both so awful.
I nourished them both when they were fledglings,   235
unable to fend for themselves. Now at my expense
she plays the cuckoo while he's a Nero.³²
They're just like the thief who repays his host
with the host's own stolen heirlooms, just like the rat
who grows fat in the grain sack, just like the viper
warmed in the bosom, like the flame in the cloth.
Savage Oedipus, envious Jupiter, they acted like this;
the one his father murdered, the other exiled.   240
At my birth, Lachesis, you gave me a hard lot,
and you spin my thread with cruel fingers.
There's no place I can safely turn;
when my own turn against me, who'll keep faith?
Oh petulant Petula, oh Fodius, foulest of foul!   245
These two are devouring all of my goods.
Very well then, I'll seek my bitter revenge.
Here's my sentence: the thief shall mount up,
and the adulteress shall be cast down —
the thief up to the gallows, the whore down to the stake —
he'll die the first and she'll follow after.
In my garden there stands an ash tree
a thousand cubits high. Beneath that tree

87

there's a cavern, and within that cave 250
there's a bottomless swamp. There Fodius,
a rope round his neck, will provide
a spectacle for the people's good pleasure;
hanging there, he'll learn what it feels like
to provide the birds with their supper.
I'll hang him myself for perhaps if another's
the hangman, there'll be some sort of deception —
the knot come loose and the villain escape.
If my knot comes undone (for you see 255
I don't really trust myself — Babio,
you always were a weakling, a real cow),[33]
and if he escapes from my rope, the tree
will hand him over to the swamp for safe-keeping.
Having escaped the Syrtes, he'll fall prey to Charybdis.
But I shall deal with Petula more mildly;
there'll be no more deceiving, once her temptation
has been removed. I shall thrash her soundly 260
but be merciful and spare her life.

[*enter Fodius*]

BABIO: Fodius, prepare for death. Give up.
Here, put this rope around your neck.

FODIUS: Why must I die?

BABIO: Anger won't let me say.
Just stand still. Let me lead you away.

FODIUS: Lead me where?

BABIO: Off to the gallows.

FODIUS: Why? You have to have a good reason
to put someone to death.

BABIO: You're Petula's lover. 265

FODIUS: That's nothing.

BABIO: Prove it, by ordeal
by fire.

FODIUS: By fire if you wish, by water
if you'd rather.

BABIO: You are her lover,
admit it.

FODIUS: I deny it.
Let me defend myself in a court of law;
no court denies anyone the right of appeal.

BABIO [*Aside*]: Fodius' good faith is apparent.
He didn't think he deserved to be punished.
Still, willows never do bear plums.   270

FODIUS: I swear by the Terean plains, by the Celean heights,[34]
I swear — take note — by the gods' stables,
Fodius is not fooling around with Petula.

BABIO: Give me your right hand as a pledge
of good faith. That's good enough for me.

FODIUS: Take it. Give me your hand too;
give me your hand as a pledge of good faith.
[*Aside*] Oh god, how easily I have escaped   275
from great danger. He knows neither
"bu" nor "ba"[35] does our Babio,
but he's a cow's tongue, is our Babio.
Fodius has just sold you a platter, and you
thought it the moon. No, Fodius isn't fooling
around with Petula; he's finished for now.
The Terean plains are not terrestrial,
nor are the Celean hills celestial.
Stables are kept for pigs and jackasses,   280
the gods' tables reserved for things more sacred.
One deceives only oneself when one swears

that it is no virtue to practice deception.
I must speak to Petula, warn her of the danger;
there's much less chance for harm
when one knows just what to expect.
[*to Petula*] I've suffered so badly, Petula,   285
that I barely escaped with my life.
Weep, pick quarrels, throw a tantrum
lest you be compelled to suffer the same.

[*enter Babio*]

PETULA: So you think I'm an adulteress, do you?
Don't give fuel to infamy's flames.
No doubt you think that the whole world,
man and woman alike, is just like yourself.
You think me to be promiscuous Thais
when I've tried so hard to be as chaste as a Sabine.
You're as debauched as that Gnatho[36] so you think   290
that I'm Thais. But you, either you're
insufferably frantic or else you're lethargic;
either you're raving insane or you've drunk
from Lethe's forgetful waters.
Your jealous mind gives you no rest;
the suspicious man knows neither hope nor repose.
Rumor is not to be trusted, for when it wants,   295
it can turn black into white, and when it wants,
it can give to the swan Memnon's ebony hue.

BABIO: I beg you, don't be so angry.
I'm only repeating what people are saying,
and most people usually confuse the wish
with the deed. I'm delighted to find
that I've been led astray by such gossip;
I like to stray — I'm happily deceived.   300

[*later*]

BABIO: My false disaster warns me to beware of

a true one; my victory today will have
a future, of that I am sure. Indulgence
can prove irresponsible, inspiring many
to sin. The goddess was slow to anger;
Niobe then grew foolhardy.[37] Petula's lamentations
do not put an end to her sins, and Fodius   305
swore many oaths; but after oaths, after promises,
the criminal returns to his same life of crime.
Who wouldn't tell lies to save his neck?
To live, no one hesitates to break his word.
Love fears nothing; love gives the orders
and error obeys. Nothing is impossible   310
for love; nothing makes it afraid.
Defeat did not extinguish Paris'
passionate flames, nor did his father's disaster,
nor Troy's destruction, not even his own.
Everyone delights in his own pleasure,
nor are the appetites of desire ever fulfilled.
Those who have once experienced the prick   315
of desire are never deterred by fear.
Moreover (and this is what alarms me the most),
those two have many opportunities for sin.
The moon is now new, but when it's full
I shall devise a new stratagem and avenge this crime.

BABIO [*to Fodius*]: I'm off to Soloe.[38] Fodius, take good care
of things while I'm gone. Be on your guard;   320
if you're not careful, the wolf will get fat
on my sheep. I'll be back as soon as I can.

FODIUS [*Aside*]: Not for a millennium or more, I hope,
and leave nothing behind but your name.

BABIO: I'll rest awhile among the bushes
here in the garden until the sun has set
in the west and the day is over.
Then I'll get up and return, protected by night;   325
then I'll have need of all my habitual guile.

FODIUS: Now it is night. Babio is away
though he hasn't gone far; he'll be home
tomorrow. We must take advantage
of this moment when all is peaceful and quiet.
May the night double her length for us,
may Titan moon provide us with a night
just as long as that which she gave
to Alcmena when Jupiter was her lover.   330

BABIO: It's midnight. Everything is dead silent.
Now everyone is safely asleep. Luck is with me.
I'm on my way. There is a window.
I'll just peek in. The moon will help me
to see. Look what I see! Fodius
isn't in his bed. They're together,   335
I just know it. What are they up to now?
I've got my trusty knife; God give me courage,
and sharpness to it. I'll catch Fodius.
Once I've caught him, he won't escape me intact;
his sling and balls will go away with me.
                         [*he sneezes*]
That's a bad omen. I sneezed once,
but the second won't come. Now I'm afraid.   340
Trivialities like these matter a lot.

FODIUS [*to Petula*]: Petula, what's going on outside?
I heard something, someone blew his nose.
Is Babio back? I'm right. It's him.
You stay quietly here in bed. I'll get up
and give him just what he's got
prepared for me. His dirty beard
will lose a few hairs and his side some blood.
        Who's that making all that noise outside?   345
Quick, it's a thief! Tile, get a move on,
he's getting away. Chamberpot, after him!
Hangdog, over here. Your beard will leave me
its fleece. Take this "welcome";
a beating will give you the rest.
Let Sir Cudgel salute him, and you, Whips,

92

take good care of his sides. He thought to disturb us, 350
did he? Well, as he's sown, so shall he reap.

BABIO: I'm Babio, spare me.

FODIUS: No you're not.
This isn't Soloe; he can't be in two places.

BABIO: I'm Babio, I've come back.

FODIUS: Why are you standing out there?

BABIO: I was resting. I didn't want
to disturb you, and see how I've been rewarded.

FODIUS: You never will learn to be careful. 350
Babio, you're your usual clever self.
You could have lost your life just now,
could easily have been killed by mistake,
and that's just what would have happened
if I hadn't felt merciful and called a halt.
[*Aside*] In fact, I was as brutal as could be.
[*Aloud*] Malefactors, we see, always come home
in tears. Those intent on deceit 360
will sooner or later end up lamenting.
Get up. Go in to bed, get some rest.
You can trust me. Forget those suspicions;
they're sure to destroy your health.
You are hunting in vain; you have gone
to all this trouble and caught nothing.
You'll find that searching for my deceit
is like looking for nodes on a bulrush.
Doves lack bile, swans lack the crow's 365
dusky hue, and bulrushes lack nodes.
So all my deeds are free from deceit.

BABIO: I'm glad I didn't do any damage;
my impotence won't matter at all once I do
get my chance. If you are able to resist

my blows, I'll give you a taste of my cunning
(it's all the same, I think, to conquer 370
by guile or by force). Put a pig in purple,
crown clay with gold; the pig will still be filthy,
the pot will still be made of mud.
There is no harmless serpent, no guileless
fox cub, nor can Fodius ever be trusted
to be free from tricks!
Two things make me unhappy: my wife 375
has lost her honor and I've lost my money.
I grieve because I've fallen into beatings
and she into sin. But now, since a month has past,
I'm delighted by the thought of a new revenge.
Now, with companions, I'll courageously
confront him and all of his tricks.
The solitary traveler is paralyzed by fear;
with companions he's more secure.
Alone I lost; with companions I'll win. 380

BABIO: Fodius, I am off to Soloe again.
I shall return in time for the orgies
of Bacchus. Be on your guard.
Take good care of my fields and my hearth.

FODIUS [*Aside*]: May those orgies of Bacchus when you say
you'll return not occur until our ass
becomes world-famous for playing the harp.
Let fate look after the house while I 385
take care of its mistress. It's only proper,
for his field must not go unplowed.

BABIO: Here come my companions. Now, here's the story.
I need your help. Necessity teaches us
how to recognize true friends. There's the road;
here are hiding places known only to me.
[*Aside*]: May this spot prove luckier for me 390
than the last one. That time I rushed in
and was overwhelmed. I brought on myself

94

nothing but sorrow and pain. The hunter
was captured; my prey carried me off.
I dug the hole and fell into it too.
I wished to deceive but was tripped up
by a deceit that equalled my own.
Now the hot south wind gives way to a cool one,   395
breezes follow gales, and laughter tears,
and good fortune will follow bad.
       I pursue the unchaste; I fight as thy champion,
chaste Diana. Protect the arms of thy warrior.
Grant my prayers, thou holy one,
thou who reigns in heaven and hell
and in the forests, thou mistress of
a triplicate realm. Grant my prayers,   400
sister of the sun, daughter of Jove.

[*to his companions*]   Get up.
Thrice the cock has cheerfully crowed.
Memnon's mother, the Dawn, urges us
to be on our way. Exhausted by sport,
Petula and Fodius are now sleeping deep.
I'll play the part of old Vulcan,
he will be Mars and she Venus.
On one side there'll be great lamentation,   405
on the other applause – applause for me
but tears for him as he bewails
the loss of two-thirds of his weapons.
March resolutely; with caution I'll guide
your attack from behind. The outcome
of every assault is always uncertain.
I'll observe all the secret hiding places,
I shall explore with my eyes and my ears;
the trap that my eyes can't perceive   410
my ears will be sure to detect.

FODIUS [*to Petula*]: I must get up; I've waited too long.
Here he comes, here Babio comes,
and he has got people with him.
        [*Aloud, pretending not to have heard a thing*]

I'm sick, I'm dying. Oh, if only Babio were back!
Even worse than death is dying unconfessed.
Alas, alas, how fragile is life's grace.   415
We are but foam, dreams, smoke, flowers,
ash, air — nothing more. Now man is here,
now he's gone. He breathes, then expires;
he flowers and fades, is born, then is snuffed out.
These events transpire in a brief instant.
I am overcome by a fever; it began
just as soon as Babio left; since then
I've been unable to move from this spot.   420

BABIO [*to his companions*]: Go home. I've won. His last hour's at hand.
This can mean nothing but death.
We've come to the burying. I've won. Go home.

FODIUS [*Aside*]: This is a pretty trick. I'm out of danger.
My enemy's deceived. He's taken
my hypocrisy for true religious piety.

BABIO: Now I am happy, rich — no king, no subject   425
is more so. Now you are dying, Fodius,
you whom I hate most of all.
As you descend, I ascend to the heights.
As you are overwhelmed, I am revived.
Your torment's my triumph; what I wanted I have.
Contrary to all expectation, I have my desire.
I embrace what I love; I have what I want.   430
Now you will weep for your former laughter.
Man of shadows, now you will have
nothing but shadows to embrace.
Now you will reap in Lethe's sad kingdom
that vile crop which here you sowed.
There you'll endure the vultures of Tityrus
or Ixion's wheel, or suffer the fate
of Tantalus, thirsting in the midst of much water.
Babio, you may go in. At last all is safe.   435
You can do what you want. This traitor has had it.
[*To Petula*] Sister, get up. Bring a cloth to wipe
the sweat from Fodius' brow for he's dying.

Get up. Hurry, Fodius is dying. Come here.

FODIUS: Wait just a minute. Not so fast, not so near.
First, I've a word or two to say 440
that you won't want to hear. An enthymeme
will prove a sufficient sophism to close
your argument, nor can you escape
bearing the brunt of my sophistication.

BABIO [*to Petula*]: Get up.

PETULA: Who are you?

BABIO: Babio.

PETULA: Which Babio?

BABIO: Your husband. I've come home.

PETULA: What are you doing here? It's a thief.
I'm lost. Oh, Fodius, help me!

FODIUS: I'm here. Who is this? 445

PETULA: A thief.

BABIO: Babio.

FODIUS: You're not Babio but a lecher, and so you'll leave
your pendulous parts here with our Fodius.

BABIO: Stop, I'm Babio.

FODIUS: It isn't time for the orgies
of Bacchus — that's when Babio will be back.
You're a lecher and you're going to pay
for your audacity.

BABIO: Look at me in the light.

97

FODIUS: We've no need for light, for I know
there's no Babio here. Now you'll be eclipsed.[39]   450
You will no longer be able to play
the tune for three parts; you'll only be able
to play in mother Cybele's band.[40]
I've no desire to inflict anything worse.

BABIO: O-h-h-h-h-h-h-h, I'm dying.

FODIUS: He's a thief. Bring lights.
Oh no, it's Babio. You boob, where did you come from?
When, wretch, will you learn?   455
Not until our ass can play the harp.
The cow is not clever, nor Babio wise.
You are really very lucky, you know,
that we didn't do you any worse harm.

BABIO: What harm could be any worse?
Is this injury not worth my tears?

FODIUS: Are you weeping over so small a loss?
I'm a skilled doctor. Such a tiny injury   460
is a trifling task to cure.

BABIO: That's easy for *you* to say, but it doesn't
agree with the proverb, "The healthy man
cannot comprehend the sufferings of the sick."
Oh, what a disgrace is an adulterous wife,
but worse, oh far, far worse
is that man who led her astray.
He's capable of every deceit in the world.
There is no evil more evil than a long   465
series of evils. No one is wary
of the risks that he runs from the serpent
he's long kept around as a pet.
My wife is the one who has robbed me,
and my servant has become my judge.
She pains, he plots; she's a wolf, he a lion.
She holds me down, he binds me tight.
She knocks me down, he throttles me.   470

She oppresses me, he beats me.
She stabs me, he grinds me down.
    Go get me a cart and driver.
Let me be carried away to holy places;
I want to conclude my past by making
a good end. Now I'll leave quickly.
I only wish I'd left sooner!

PETULA: You're not going to leave us so soon?

BABIO: I'd rather run away than suffer any more.

FODIUS: Weep, oh you household. Weep, oh Petula.   475
Babio is going to become a monk. Weep one and all.
[*Aside*] And don't come back till I call.
[*Aloud*] Oh brother Babio, your departure makes me so sad.
[*Aside*] I weep because I'm overcome with joy.

BABIO: Fodius, see, I give you Petula.
Now you've got what you wanted — enjoy it!
But learn from my lessons, fear my fate.   480
Farewell, Croceus and Viola, and farewell to you two.
May your life, your children, your wealth
make you happy, but Babio is here to bear witness —
pay strict attention to his parting words —
wives, children, servants — not a one's to be trusted!

Notes to *Babio*

1. Translated from the edition of Andrea Dessì Fulgheri (ed. Bertini, II).

2. This argument is found only in MS D, Oxford, Bodleian Library, Digby 53, from the end of the 12th or the beginning of the 13th century.

3. A statement which argues against considering Rumor (*Fama*) as a speaking part (see n. 31), although the qualification "principal" suggests that perhaps Rumor was, like Croceus' companions (non-speaking parts, however), not considered major.

4. *Sacerdos* in Latin; there is no indication whatever that Babio was a priest or that he had any inclinations in that direction before his final encounter with Fodius. The "Argument," however, is insistent on this point.

5. The manuscript reading is corrupt; Croceus is meant.

6. *Miles*, the customary medieval Latin for "knight," instead of the classical *eques*.

7. The word here is plural, although only one dog, Melampus, is mentioned in the play.

8. Faral (1948) suggests that these lines are a parodic imititation of the opening of *Pamphilus*.

9. The name of one of Actaeon's hounds in Ovid, *Metamorphoses* 3.206, 208.

10. In Aristotelian philosophy, that which is indivisible (*individuus*) is immobile (*Physics* 6.12-16; 8.6).

11. An echo of Ovid, *Heroides* 12.61, "Hinc amor, hinc timor est; ipsum timor auget amorem" (On this side love, on that fear; fear increases love itself).

12. Phyllis, a name popular in the Middle Ages, comes from Ovid, *Heroides* 2; also *Ars. Amatoria* 3.37, *Remedia Amoris* 55, etc. (she died for love of Demophoon). Thais was a common name for a promiscuous woman. The original Thais was a celebrated Athenian courtesan; the name occurs in Ovid, *A.A.* 3.604, *R.A.* 383, Terence, *Eunuchus* 1.2.11. See also the "Life of Thais" (a repentant prostitute) contained in the *Vitae Patrum*. The reading of MSS *CP,* "Thetis," and adopted by Mozley, is what Babio probably meant to say, but, as Bate suggests in his note, this is another instance of Babio's confusion ("Babio can be relied upon to make mistakes when parading his erudition").

13. A reference to Ovid, *Amores* 1.5.9, "Ecce Corinna venit, tunica velata recincta" (Behold Corinna comes, her covering tunic unbelted).

14. Babio is playing on the two names as common names of flowers.

15. The crocus was traditionally a symbol of power and nobility (see Faral, 1948, p. 8).

16. This line involves two jokes; I take *salvo sexu* to mean that Babio isn't a eunuch, but Chevallier (p. 46) translates, "sans que mon sexe en souffre." *Subdar,* "to go beneath," plays on two senses, literal and social, of position.

17. An untranslatable pun; *plus pene potens* means "nearly more powerful," but *pene potens* suggests as well potent with respect to the penis (see Bate's note).

18. The name of a boxer in Vergil, *Aeneid* 5.387, 460.

19. The name is a play on *vasa vorans* (see Bate's note) with *B* and *V* pronounced identically.

20. Babio's grammatical errors are untranslatable. His *sedite* (for the correct *sedete*) might have sounded, suggest Fulgheri and Bate, like *cedite* "give way."

21. Compare the jokes in *Geta* about proving that Socrates is an ass.

22. The attribution of these lines in the MSS differ: in *C* they are given to Fodius, in *L*, which Faral followed, to Petula, and in *D* (wrongly) to Babio.

23. Not to be taken literally; it is the equivalent of "friend."

24. Babio's choice of weapon and position in battle recalls that of Geta.

25. This line probably contains, again pun on *pene* "almost," and *pene*, ablative of penis (above, n. 17).

26. Another echo of *Geta* 489-90.

27. Plays on grammatical terms with erotic *double entendre* were common in Latin medieval literature; see, for example, Pittaluga, 1979, 147-50.

28. Parody of the language and arguments of scholasticism; compare *Geta* 395 ff.

29. Another pun on *pene* (above, n. 17).

30. *Livia*, the wife of Augustus, is my conjecture for the MS "Libia" (cf. the frequent confusion between *v* and *b* in medieval Latin). Chevallier conjectures "Lidia," which would be a reference to the "heroine" of Arnulf of Orléans' scabrous comedy *Lidia*. Since the other allusions all involve references to ancient Rome, I consider "Livia" more likely. "Marcia," while not referring to any specific Roman heroine, recalls such stern old Romans as Marcus Porcius Cato.

31. The attribution of these lines is confused in the MSS; Fulgheri here follows the *didascalia* of *P*, *Fama Babioni*, which is confirmed by *C*. Other MSS assign the lines to Babio. I here depart from Fulgheri because of the use of first person pronouns, which are awkward if Rumor speaks the lines.

32. Nero: because like the emperor, Fodius may be thought of as having sexual relations with his "mother" (mistress); see Bate's note *ad loc.*

33. Although the MSS attribute this remark to Babio, Fulgheri notes

that it could well be an aside by Fodius, who has been listening to his master's tirade.

34. Fodius' false oaths cannot be reproduced satisfactorily in English; Babio mistakes "Terean" (from Tereus) for *terre* 'earth,' and "Celei" as *celi* 'heaven.' He confuses ăras 'pigsties' with āras 'altars.' *Fŏdit* means '*is* copulating' while *fŏdit* means '*has* copulated.'

35. A medieval proverb; cf. William IX of Aquitaine, 5.26.

36. The parasite in Terence's *Eunuchus*.

37. Cf. Ovid, *Metamorphoses* 6.146 ff.

38. City in Cilicia noted for the bad speech of its inhabitants, whence the word 'solecism'; as Bate points out, it is an ideal place for Babio to visit.

39. Literally, "Now you will be an eclipse." Bate notes that the term *eclipsis* is used by Nigel Wireker in his *Speculum Stultorum* to mean "impotence."

40. Followers of Cybele were known for self-castration.

ALDA[1]

by William of Blois

THE ARGUMENT

Alda perishes in childbirth. Ulfus transfers
his love from his wife to his daughter,
playing for her the mother's role
as well as the father's. Lest any man see her,
or she any man, her father locks the girl up,
but Pyrrhus falls in love with her,
captivated by her reputation. His servant
deceives him, his old nurse gives him aid.   5
The girl, although locked up, learns
that the fictitious woman is male.
She conceives. Her father complains.
But at last, discovering the author
of the deception, he makes him his
son-in-law. The action is pleasing.

THE AUTHOR'S PROLOGUE

After I had mocked in my verse
the quarrel between the flea and the fly,[2]
the tale of the "Man-Become-Maid"   10
offers itself to my pen (I've had to use
a substitute title instead of the real one —
the correct name would not scan in my meter).[3]
This play was a recent import, ravished
from Menander's bosom, and already translated
into Latin — a shabby job, however, unidiomatic,
couched in the crude language of the common folk,   15
although very elegant in its poet's native Greek.
Since, therefore, the play sought the attention
of a new comic poet to replace its Menander,
I thought to offer myself in Menander's stead,
although I am unequal to such a great task
and the subject matter lies far beyond me —   20

104

people will accuse me of having depicted
cypress trees instead of a shipwreck [4]
and charge that my muse has gone astray.
I've had to transcend the role of comic poet;
my comedy oversteps its boundaries,
mixing words not proper to the genre
with the appropriate level of diction.
A modest reader may find the vocabulary too salacious,   25
but that is the subject's fault, not mine;
lest I make a whore speak like a chaste Sabine matron,
I've had to employ the words my subject demands.

[*The Tale*]

    Ulfus, embracing his wife who is about
to give birth, complains of the gods whose anger
has caused him great harm. "The only man,"   30
Ulfus says, "who is truly prosperous
is the man who knows no prosperity.
It is no misfortune to be unfortunate,
for those who have nothing cannot be harmed
by the wrath of a wrathful deity.
It is no misfortune to be unfortunate,
for those to whom chance has conceded nothing   35
have no concessions to beg from deaf Jove.
It is no misfortune to be unfortunate,
for the unfortunate man has nothing so dear
that its loss can make him less fortunate;
he has no joy, he who thinks himself joyful,
nor is he wretched whom we think wretched.   40
The happy man stands upright and fears to fall;
the poor man lies low and, while waiting
to rise higher, has nowhere to fall.
Hard pressed by adversity, the poor man
fears nothing but waits securely
until fortune's wheel turns once again
and raises him up. But he whom happiness favors
has for his inseparable companions   45
sleepless anxiety, which makes him grow thin,

105

and terror, which always torments him.
True prosperity, therefore, consists in
prosperity's absence, for grief springs
from prosperity and from nothing else.
I know this well from experience, for that
which just now is the source of all joy
has become the source of all grief.   50
Alda, my companion, dear companion of my joy,
            [*A line is missing*]
Look now how all my fortunes have altered.
Grief turns all my pleasure to pain.
While you lived I was happy; happier   55
should I be if I could die with you.
Alas, fate would have been more merciful
if less mercifully it had measured out
for us threads that were equal in length.
Then neither would feel harm when both
were harmed; equal in grief
we would know no grief at all.   60
Just as oneness of mind and of spirit
has made us one, so should one single day
have carried the two of us off.
Where are you going without me, my best part,
my dear love? Am I to go on living
without you, I who am your best part?"

        As he spoke, tears of tender love   65
flooded his face. And Alda comforts
her husband's tears in this fashion:
"Why, my faithful companion, have you fallen
into such feminine softness? Will you,
by your tears, deny that you are a man?
Your grief increases mine; your tears
cause my body even more pain. Stop weeping,   70
I beg you; check your sighs. Tears and
lamentation will not call me back.
If your tenderness, your compassion, for me
is truly strong, if our love is indeed
true love — then dying, loving, I pray you,   75
grant them the joy of a joyful fulfillment.

106

Remember that you are the author of my grief,
as well as its subject. May my suffering move you,
but let it not move you to such effeminate grief —
no, for then you'd be unable to do what I ask.   80
As the experience of my childbed will prove,
to you a daughter will be born as I die;
the gods have perceived it would be a crime
for them to separate two whom such a love,
such an equal love, unites as one.
Therefore they make us amends, admit their guilt;   85
they have assessed your loss and make restitution.
If the jealous fates have taken this Alda from you,
they will give you back an equal or better
Alda. The gods in their goodness have
preserved me for you in our mutual child,
and though I may die, I shall still survive   90
in my child. I die before my time,
but my life's root has sprouted into
a new plant, increasing in my child.
Ulfus, my essence is transferred
into another, a better Alda
who appropriates my days for herself.
I am transformed, not dead.   95
I am transfused into another body
made from our bodies. She'll be a part of me,
she who dwelt first in her father,
then flowed from father to mother,
an unformed mass, a crude ball.
She is equally ours; we live equally in her,
and through her I shall be even dearer to you.   100
My good husband, may your loving heart
receive this child offered to you
from her mother's loving body.
I entrust her to you; through her I am entrusted
to you and in your wife's place receive
your daughter. So that you need not
live without me, I shall live on,   105
surviving in her, and thus I am preserved
although the fates have carried me off.
Let her know a mother's love from her father,

107

and for her mother's sake, play the
mother's role too. May she succeed me,
inheriting my love, and let that love
which joined me to you, join her to you.   110
Show her that you are, I beg — Oh Lucina,
help me! — a tender fa-father, and be,
I entreat you, a mother in father's guise."
    She spoke, and through her tears could hardly
pronounce, "fa-arewell." The daughter
comes into the light; the mother departs.

    Joyous and sad, Ulfus grieves and is happy;   115
as husband he has cause for tears, as father
for laughter; he pays a high price
for fatherhood — the loss of his wife;
he ceases to be a husband just as
he becomes a father. But the daughter
redeems and makes up for her mother's death,
and her father receives her as if in her mother's stead.   120

    Little by little the daughter steals
away her mother's memory and makes
her father forget his wife.
All his affection is focused on Alda
(for this is her name — she is named for
her mother). What zeal, what hard work   125
did Nature put into Alda's creation!
The splendor of her face bears true witness
and teaches us. Her fair skin
would have been like the white snow,
her complexion like roses, did she not
far surpass both roses and snow.
On the maiden's face the rosy lily
is painted; on her cheeks blushing   130
pink glows, snowy white gleams.
Her eyebrow's delicate arch is a crown
to her laughing eyes; her hair
could pass for gold, and her lovely lips,
like delicate roses, invite sweet kissing —

lips which an industrious nature has artfully   135
modeled into a delicate fullness
just to receive her fill of kisses.

From her infancy her father guards her
devotedly, keeping her from seeing
or talking to any other man.
Her father's concern embellishes and molds
her mind, adorning it with virtue's beauty.   140
He impresses a matron's deportment
upon the tender maiden, checking her
lightheartedness with a mature gravity.
He unites discordant elements
with a harmonious compact, befriending
all that opposes him, and making it
compliant by his firm opposition.
Firmness he imparts to the fragile sex,   145
uniting gravity with youth, modesty
with beauty. Her youth endures this constraint,
nor is it permitted to follow its dictates;
she cannot pursue her youthful whims.
Beauty is much amazed to find modesty
as its companion; constancy is dumbfounded   150
to find itself thriving in a woman.

Alda is grown up, at the marriageable age,
but she has never seen any man but her father.
But however jealously her father's
fearful anxiety might keep the sight
of such beauty from public view,
locks form no impediment to gossip.   155
Locked up though Alda might be, gossip
can unlock all locks. Gossip
keeps Alda's name on people's lips;
people make of Alda a legend, and a true
one to boot. Her beauty, in fact,
far surpasses its reputation; it is
a miracle they talk of. No, the tales
are untrue — the tales tell less than the truth!   160

    Such tales of Alda's miraculous beauty
stir Pyrrhus' heart. Pyrrhus is not
inferior to Alda in breeding;
they are equal in age, their fathers
are equal in wealth, but an unequal
spirit separates this pair of equals.

    Pyrrhus falls in love with what he's heard;   165
he burns with blind passion, but he does not know
what he loves so insanely; he does not know
what he loves, for he loves the girl
for her reputation and not for herself.
Thus he loves — no, not loves, but is mad with love.

    Pyrrhus had a servant named Spurius
(indeed the name was a veritable omen).[5]   170
His hair, like filthy wool, was perpetually
matted with mange, a solid mass
as if it were only a single hair.
Constant drowsiness and a tangled thicket
of eyebrows disfigure eyes buried deep
beneath his brow. His goatlike snout   175
seems broken by some injury; the flattened
nose does not project out from his cheeks.
His swollen lips bulge out from his great
gaping maw, a deep cavernous hollow.
The stench which issues from his nostrils
infects and befouls the atmosphere
far worse than that which comes from   180
a lower part. His belly sticks out
far in front, his butt far behind;
Spurius follows along slowly after
the former, dragging the latter behind.
His belly preceding, his butt coming after,
so he goes on his way. Therefore
he both follows and precedes his body.
Nothing suffices to fill the abyss   185
of his great belly, a void fatal to both
Bacchus and Ceres. And as he goes,
he iambicks along, for with his short steps

he makes iambics (one leg is long,
the other is short). His legs, he maintains,
get their russet hue from campaign boots —
their redness, in fact, is due   190
to fireside campaigning. He is shod
with yesterday's mud added to that
of today — to protect his feet from the cold.

    Pyrrhus implores his aid, revealing
the cause and content of all his grief.
Spurius says to himself, "Take care,   195
good Jupiter, that this fellow remain
thus hare-brained for a very long time,
oh please do! Now all doors will be open
for me, and I won't even have to steal
the keys. Now at last Spurius is going
to get enough to eat. Now, Spurius,
you'll have need for new guile.
Dissemble, Spurius, dissemble, and you'll have
the sort of food your stomach prefers.   200
Now you'll be freed from the starvation
which your master's tight purse-strings
have caused you to suffer.

    "Don't be afraid, Pyrrhus; I'll watch
over you," Spurius says aloud. "I'll carry out
all your wishes. But if the pupil   205
does not obey, the master's teachings
come to naught, and he has sown
his seed in barren ground. My guile
and my labor will suffer that fate
if you refuse to trust my advice."

    "Instruct me," says Pyrrhus, "for I am prepared
to obey; I hang on your every word   210
of good advice or command."

    The servant is delighted to hear this.
"You know, dear boy, you know that everyone,
the gods included, adores getting gifts.

Alda

Whoever propitiates the gods with gifts
finds them not deaf but favorable
to his requests. But he who doesn't   215
bribe Jupiter with gold, who comes empty-handed,
will offer prayers empty of answers.
With Jupiter, a gift makes honorable
the dishonorable cause; it frees the guilty,
imprisons the innocent. With Jupiter,
piety's image is up for sale;
crime is concealed with purchased piety.   220
The gods give nothing away gratis,
and everything is very expensive.
Great gifts buy only small rewards.
Why the gods even put their holy temples
on the market, and Jupiter himself
sells his pontificate. The gods' grace
is for sale. You can't have grace gratis;   225
it's only for the buyer with a great deal to spend.
Admission to the temple is also for sale,
and the priest forbids the empty-handed
to gain admission to Jove. No one gives
gratis because no one gets gratis.
Everyone sells because someone else   230
has made him pay. Grace displayed for sale
like this is just like a prostitute;
reduced to the level of a shameful ware,
it debases its buyers as well.
In short, the overpowering desire
for profit puts a price on everything.
There's nothing that money can't buy.
        "You may wonder where this digression   235
is leading; I may seem to you
to have strayed from far from my path.
Pay attention to my drift, to where
I am headed, and to what my roundabout
speech intends; it is not irrelevant
to your cause. For just as the gods
cannot be swayed without gifts,
neither can a girl be won without presents.   240
Girls are docile in following bad examples;

112

and love of gifts, which puts a price
on everything else, puts one on them too.
A woman does not inquire about
her lover's family, his beauty, or morals;
no, her first question concerns the price
that he is willing and able to pay.
She loves the gift, not the giver;   245
she measures his love by his gifts —
her lover is loved just as much as he gives.
That's why I've lost all my value
in Spurca's eyes; I've nothing left
for sale but my toga. Send, therefore,
some gift to Alda to enchant her,
to steal into her heart, to win her for you.   250
Let's send her a fine *pâté en croûte*
as the first token of your devotion.
It will be a very fine omen,
and Alda can be won by such measures.
I shall include some words to torment her;
from our meal she'll nourish new fires.
But you must be extravagant
in your first gift; let the first gift   255
create a good hope for the future.
Thus she'll be bound to you by twin chains —
by your presents and my poetry.
A stingy lover is neither praiseworthy
nor lovable. Be extravagant!"

     "But I've nothing," says Pyrrhus.   260

     And Spurius: "I know, I know, dear boy;
I know that your father's impropriety
does not permit you to behave
properly. The stinginess of our stern,
our severe old man — oh the shame! —
why it makes you behave as if you were
a stodgy old man instead of a lad.
Enjoy yourself! Be an active lover,   265
just as you should be at your age.
Don't lose any sleep over old men's morals

113

before you've grown old. When your coffers are empty,
why are your father's stuffed to the brim?
If the father is rich, can the son really
be poor? Deceive the old man.
We'll make a duplicate key and break in."

     Pyrrhus does so and repairs the state   270
of his coffers. Spurius takes the money
and makes a splendid *pâté*.
He gives the orders, he carries them out.
First he raises the dough up in the shape
of a cone, then kneads it down flat
with his fingers. Placing one hand   275
on the pastry, he turns it around
and around, enlarging it and then
compressing it into a ball. On all sides
he builds up a continuous wall,
flaring the pastry out into curved bays.
Industriously he sweats over his task;
a new breed of potter, he shapes   280
a capacious vase. He cuts up chickens
and puts in some pork to add richness,
as if to fatten the mixture. His capacious
invention he fills with meat arranged
in just the right order, each kind
keeping to its own assigned place.
Pepper forms the first layer which serves   285
as a foundation, then the meat,
over which he scatters great quantities
of fine seasoning powder. The top
he covers with crust like a roof;
another twisted piece of crust
surrounds the sides to bind them up fast.

     Spurius departs, and Pyrrhus entreats him
to bear extravagant greetings, innumerable prayers.   290
But Spurius thinks to himself, "Spurius,
let's celebrate a holiday today
since everything's turned out far better
than you dared to hope. Before today

I've had nothing but the crust of *pâté*
to eat; now I shall eat the whole thing
myself. Crusts have always been   295
my portion, and do you know why?
Because crusts don't agree with the teeth
of that old soldier, my master.
Moreover, he doesn't abandon the crust to me
before he's struggled a long time to chew it;
by this ruse he thought to crack my teeth.
Well, right now I'm going to be merciful
to my poor teeth and give them only
the tender heart of the *pâté* to chew.   300
This *pâté* will reknot, will rekindle
Spurca's love and will restore
you to her good graces again.
She'll receive you with smiles, she who
shut you out when your purse was flat,
filled only with profitless air."

      In the poorest neighborhood, in the worst   305
slum of the city, the broken-down house
of Spurca⁶ stands, an utter ruin.
A scraggy wicker fence of thorns
guards the door; the whole hovel
is held together by only three ropes.
Spurca is seated at home, alone
and disheveled; she is devouring   310
the entrails of some old sow, seasoned
only with coarse salt, and drinking
the remains of yesterday's broth
that she'd scrounged up somewhere.

      Spurius enters. She glances at him
askance; lightning flashes in her eyes,
and seizing a weapon, she falls on him.
The blows come thick and fast.
"Get out, hangdog, get out," she screams.   315
But then he reveals the sacred object
he's carrying; respect for that holy thing
calms her down; her anger cools.

He is restored to her good graces;
their quarrel is wholly forgotten.

    The two banqueters sit solemnly down
at the table, a little stool balanced 320
precariously on only three legs.
Spurius makes it a festive occasion
with wine which he has stolen, and Spurca
brings out the holiday cup. Three times
it had been broken and three times
stitched up — the shoemaker and his coarse needle
had been its surgeon, and he covered
the ends of his threads by smearing them 325
over with dirty wax and black pitch.

    They get up from dinner. Spurca prepares
her bed — a small pile of straw — for her lover.
She spreads a cloth over the straw,
but age and consuming poverty 330
have worn it quite out. It bears many wounds;
many a scar disfigures that squalid
rag — the entire thing was nothing
but patches or holes. It is disintegrating;
scarcely one part adheres to another.
The rotten weaving can barely sustain
its own weight. Such is the bed 335
which receives them both. There is only a sack
to serve for a blanket to cover them,
and it is only a very partial
covering, for it covers one part
and leaves the other part bare.
Spurca curls herself up into a ball, 340
heels pressed into her backside,
her knees drawn up to her cheeks.
Spurius, however, is somewhat less pliant;
he's burdened down by his belly and cannot
employ the same ruse. When his flanks are covered,
his feet freeze and beg the flanks
to have pity. The flanks share their cover,
but they too freeze, so the feet, 345

116

though unwilling, have to give back the cover.
This skimpy arrangement causes great pain
to their sides, as much from the ground's hardness
as from the cold. The rocky soil
impresses its rocks right up into them,
and like a seal, engraves itself   350
onto their sides. The left side runs
to the aid of its brother, the right;
they have to lie on the left side
until the right recovers from its pain.
The straw furrows their flesh into folds
and sticks to them as if born there —
the skin conceals the buried straw.
The cloth sheet on the bottom,   355
already sadly unraveled by age,
cannot keep the straw in its proper place.

       Spurius gets up in the morning, bristling
with straw; his head bears away its bed
like a trophy; 'tis a most pernicious
guest who departs, stealing away
with him the very bed he's slept in.

       He goes home to find Pyrrhus and says,   360
"Pyrrhus, my skin is quite worn out
with whippings; how many blows, poor me,
did I receive and how many threats!
Unfortunately I was discovered to be
a go-between and was captured there,
right on her doorstep; your girl did not
get a taste of our food. Sigh for another;   365
you'll get nowhere with Alda, I fear."

       He finished his speech. But love torments
poor Pyrrhus all the more cruelly.
No hope offers solace to his desires;
his plans seem to offer no chance of success.
But in a boy hope never lies dormant;
hopelessness adds oil to his fires,   370
dry wood to his flames. The more he sees

117

everything going against his desire,
the more fiercely love, that cruelest disease,
is consumed with passion; his face
reflects his poor consumed heart —
he's nothing but skin drawn tight over bones.

Now Pyrrhus, it happens, has a sister;   375
in the sister's face is much of the brother
and much of the brother appears in the sister's.
Thus the sister wears her brother's appearance
and the brother the sister's; only their sex
distinguishes one from the other. But now
sex is no longer the sole mark of distinction,
for the lover's complexion grows languid.   380
It is the lover who languishes and not
the love — love's power cannot grow languid,
for the lover's languor is active and strong.
His insanity feeds on his insane languor;
love increases the more the lover pines away.

Pyrrhus' old nurse continually urges   385
the boy with her tears, with her prayers,
to tell her the cause of his suffering.
With difficulty, by tears and entreaties,
she twists his secret out of him —
whom, why, how much, and how madly he loves.
The old woman withdraws into the secret
recesses of her crafty mind; collecting
her thoughts, she thinks long and hard.   390
An old woman's shrewdness is exceptionally fertile;
she sorts things out and discovers
just what she might do for poor Pyrrhus.

Alda's faithful friend, her dearest companion,
is Pyrrhus' sister — that very sister who,
had she not been a woman, would have been Pyrrhus.
Her father had entrusted her to Alda,   395
so Alda might teach her good morals.
The nurse summons this girl from Alda's chamber
as if there had been some business at home.

118

She makes the brother and sister exchange
their clothing, so brother and sister
are disguised as each other. Thus garbed   400
in man's clothing the girl becomes male,
and in woman's clothing the man becomes female.
Even taking good note of every detail,
the nurse can barely detect the disguise —
the ruse nearly fools its inventor.
She nearly thinks that Pyrrhus honestly   405
is a girl, that her deception isn't deceit.
She carefully shows the boy how and why
and what he should do, and to whom and when
he should speak, and in what way.
So instructed, he departs, fearful and hopeful,
considering what might transpire,
trembling with terror mixed with desire.   410
He softens his gait, he makes his stride
feminine; with smaller steps he minces along.

He reaches the desired chamber
(Alda is kept hidden away in a room
buried deep within the house).
Alda is cleansing the wool weighed out,   415
spinning it fine and filling the spindle
with new threads. She wonders what has delayed
her friend's return — a boyfriend, not girlfriend,
that's what Pyrrhus is returning her.
At first sight of her, he stands frozen still,
and in a stupor the lover adores
the divine face he longed for so fiercely.   420
He stands still, his eyes glued on her,
and though he tries, he cannot recall
himself from her. He is enchanted.
The beauty which blooms on the maid's tender
face beguiles his greedy eyes.
Pyrrhus at last recalls his unwilling eyes —   425
they nearly refuse and turn back their gaze,
indignant at being removed.
The maid would have perceived all of this,
but her innocence aids the deception.

119

Pyrrhus comes nearer. With great difficulty
he refrains from stealing sweet kisses,   430
with great difficulty conceals the fact
that he is a man. Whenever fair Alda
begins to speak, he places his mouth
near hers to drink her words from her lips.
The place is auspicious, the occasion promises
a successful conclusion to his deception,
so Pyrrhus says, "I would prove to be   435
a disloyal girlfriend to my dearest friend
if I should begrudge you the fruit of my knowledge;
therefore I want you to learn what
I have just learned. I want to share
something my nurse, concerned for my welfare,
has just taught me. You must not neglect
to practice most often that which I teach you,
and then when you die, you'll not die   440
completely; the greater part of you
will survive; you'll live on after death."

    Alda naively promises to be obedient
and insists he do just what he promised.

    "Lest my demonstration be sterile or fruitless,"[8]   445
Pyrrhus says, "model your actions on mine.
Do what I do; let your actions
give their assistance to mine, and let
your desire be united with mine."

    He knots her then in a passionate embrace,
and putting his arms round her shoulders,   450
gathers the maiden close to his bosom.
And she just the same puts her arms about him
and hangs from the noble youth's shoulders.
As many kisses — and of like quality —
as he gives, so many does he receive;
she is no less passionate than he.
If he nibbles her lips with tender bites,   455
he receives an equal number of nibbles.
They drink in each other's lips and suck them;

they wantonly enjoy their mutual kissing.
Perfect equality reigns. Their playful tongues
take turns in visiting each other,
then inviting the other into their homes.   460
Joyfully each arises to welcome the visitor
and offers it the hearth's hospitality.
And while they thus wrestle with one another
(a private, a pleasurable contest),
tongue ties tongue tight together
in a friendly embrace. After Pyrrhus
has taken enough kisses, he takes all the rest — 9   465
he enjoys her virginity's flower.
Finally Alda feels the frequent, panting blow
of his rod, and notes carefully each detail,
and when she's abandoned herself to Venus' joys,
she asks herself just what is that thing,
rather like a tail or some strange swelling,   470
and how can anything quite so rigid
give her such pleasure. As she marvels, she says,
"You were dear to me before, but now most dear;
before you were my faithful companion,
but now you've become my faithful
school-mistress. Thanks to your services
though I shall die, I shall still live   475
and shall survive even after my death.
What reward can I give you which is worthy
of your most kind demonstration?
No thanks of mine can equal your services.
Repeat the demonstration, I beg you;
repeat it again and again, so I
can better remember it. If you will repeat it   480
ten times, those ten repetitions will please 10
me most greatly — indeed nothing could give me
more pleasure. That instrument you have taught me
to use with such pleasure, tell me,
where can I get one? What is it?
Where does it come from, tell me,   485
that hard swelling rising up from your groin,
that . . . sort of tail that you work so hard?"

121

Her naive question makes Pyrrhus laugh.
He answers her with a pleasant fiction.
"Learn, my faithful friend, what this tail is   490
and where it comes from — this swelling of my groin —
what it is and where it comes from.
Recently a new merchant came to the city
with many tails like this one for sale.
The whole city gathered in the market place
(girls especially thronged the square),
and I was the first to be overcome
with desire for this new merchandise.
Their prices varied according to weight;   495
big ones were expensive, small ones cost less.
I bought a small one since I hadn't much money,
and that's what labored so hard in your service.
It did what it could but had it been bigger,
it could have pleased you even more.   500
First it extends itself proudly, swollen hard,
then subsides and shrinks down, nearly pulled off.
When it's ready to wrestle, it seeks out
a companion for battle; the game it played
with you was for it a desperate struggle.
Therefore after such blows coming thick and fast,
such sweaty battles (it sweats all over),   505
it is exhausted by toil. Then, poor thing,
it suffers a certain shrinking, and with a tremor
pays its conqueror the tribute it owes.
Then the swelling subsides. Its rigid pride,
once so haughty, hangs down its head;
the tail hangs limp, withdraws into itself."   510

These words make Alda groan deeply;
she immediately answers his speech with her own.
"Alas, my friend, you were too parsimonious.
You would have been poor but happy
had you bought the biggest of tails."

They continue in the sweet enjoyments   515
of Venus for seven whole days (and seven
nights too). Pyrrhus promises a swift

122

repetition, lest sorrow follow their joy,
or severity their delight. Then he goes home.
He bears sure signs of his victory —   520
his face reveals a new wantonness,
his smile reflects his happy spirit.
On his face, now peaceful with joy, one can read
the happy state of his heart. His face
betrays his heart, and his old nurse rejoices,
triumphant at the success of her trick.

    By now the sister has removed   525
her brother's clothes and he hers;
the brother is no longer his sister
nor is she disguised as her brother.
But Alda's belly is growing larger,
and as it increases, it reveals her crime.
An unaccustomed burden distends her belly.
She herself laughs at the crime of her belly's
increase, nor will she believe
that there was vice in her vicissitude.   530
She laughs at her father's "mendacity"
(really "veracity") when he accused her
of talking to a man, and touching one too.
She swears that she has never known
a man, not even by name,
and she deceives him, but innocently.
She truthfully swears that his truth   535
is untrue; her naiveté saves the ruse
from certain discovery. Thus neither
of them is telling a lie
(thanks to her innocence), although
what she denies he swears is true.

    When he finds he's laboring in vain,
the man addresses himself and complains: 540
"Whoever thinks he can forbid the sea's waves
to rise and fall or the fire to burn
deceives himself. Even more disgracefully
demented is the man who thinks to rule
a woman's levity by his grave councils.

There can never be bricks without mud,   545
a serpent without venom, nor bile without
its bitter smell. Nor can the feminine sex
unlearn the vice which is inherent in it,
nor will any woman long remain chaste.
Moreover, a girl can't even associate
with other girls, for one of them
will turn herself into a man.   550
Here's a memorable example to add
to the list: my daughter has been made pregnant
by a maid-become-man. I don't know whether
my son-in-law (daughter-in-law should I say?),[11]
will be masculine, feminine, or neuter.
I did not expect to have a son-in-law   555
of the feminine gender. I've been wounded
by an enemy I did not even suspect."

    Chatterbox Gossip picks up all the details
from his lips and fills the greedy
ears of the city with the story.
Gossip attacks the sister of Pyrrhus,
slandering her, blaming her for Pyrrhus' crime,
and calling her a hermaphrodite.   560
When Pyrrhus hears of Gossip's error —
the crime of which his sister is falsely
accused — he reveals his deception and clears
her name, restoring her good reputation.

    The action is pleasing. The two guilty ones   565
receive praise, and Alda marries her deceiver.

Notes to *Alda*

1. Text from the edition of Wintzweiller, in Cohen, I, pp. 131-151.

2. A reference to William's *Pulicis et musce iurgia.*

3. The *Mascula Virgo,* by which phrase William translates Menander's *Androgynos.* The few fragments which have survived of this work bear no resemblance to the *Alda;* Menander's plays are far more decorous.

4. A reference to Horace, *Ars Poetica* 19-21. According to a Greek anecdote retold by Horace, a painter whose specialty was cypress trees offered to include this tree in a painting depicting a shipwreck.

5. The Latin *spurius* has the same meaning as its English cognate.

6. The name of Spurius' girlfriend means "vile, dirty, filthy."

7. Traditionally in these works, the go-between's first approach does not succeed (cf. *Pamphilus* and *Lidia*). Here Spurius, who of course never tried to reach Alda, relies on this convention.

8. In the Vienna manuscript, a prudish hand has erased lines 445-513.

9. A quotation from Ovid, *Ars Amatoria* 1.669, where Ovid maintains that the lover who stops with kisses is a fool who deserves to lose his advantage.

10. A particularly playful allusion to Horace, who wrote in *Ars Poetica* 365: "Haec placuit semel, haec deciens repetita placebit," (this pleased only once; that, though repeated ten times, will please).

11. William has wittily invented a feminine *genera* for the masculine *gener* "son-in-law."

LIDIA[1]

By Arnulf of Orléans

The Argument

After my muse first laughed at the sportive knight,[2]
she inspired my mind yet a second time.
So that my *Adventures of Lidia,*[3] imitated from works of old,
might find approval, I have here depicted
all the feminine wiles worthy of note.
I have shown all that a woman is capable of   5
so you may flee forewarned:[4] after all,
you too may have a Lidia in your life.

The Prologue

Whoever is not familiar with Pearus[5]
and the pears fallen from the pear tree,
smiles when he hears *Geta*[6] and is overcome by laughter;
but will anyone be amazed at Jupiter's deceit
or the crimes committed by gods if he recalls
Lidia and what she is capable of doing?   10
Who will marvel at Amphitryon, deceived by Jupiter
only once, when Lidia deceived Decius four times?
Amphitryon, moreover, believed that nothing was something,
while Decius believed that what he saw was nothing.
A suitable ruse deceived them both with an equal deceit;   15
tricked, each of them thought deceit no deceit.
   Jealous one,[7] you there growing pale, who denies
that these little horns are a subject for laughter?
The color that gleams in these fine feathers is mine.
   Jealous one, don't go sneaking around, and watch
what you say: slander increases and spreads shame abroad.   20
   Jealous one, in case you don't know, reason isn't confined
to one man alone; several can have it by dint of hard work.
   The father of the Heliades[8] enriched himself with wings,
and wished for long life for the phoenix.

126

The parrot, more powerful in one important respect,   25
is far from envious of such birds as these
for he alone can imitate human speech.
If hard work and long study have made Homer
number one among the Greeks, yet has a muse
the equal of his inspired our Vergil,
a bard not inferior in art or in reason.   30

The Story Begins

Pearus is a knight, Decius is a duke,
and Lidia is his wife; the first is loyal
to the stern duke while the woman is fickle.
But what is the good of severity, of loyalty?
A woman steals away fidelity with deceit and
gravity with guile. By art, deceit, study,
she steals, she seduces, she ensnares;   35
a woman becomes the virus that destroys virility.[9]
In a woman, madness rages more fiercely;
it threatens more unsettlingly; it is
headstrong and intolerant of any delay.
When the illicit gives pleasure, the lawful is
quickly sent packing, and when all shame is
removed, crime increases with the aid of guile.   40

Lidia stands, she sinks down, she wanders and
grows weak; hope, shame, guile, fickleness,
and blind love — all drive her now hither, now thither.
Whenever she is sitting beside the duke and Pearus
chances to pass, she leans on the duke's shoulder,
seeming to faint. In her conversation
part of Pearus's name often sticks in her throat: 45
the first half is heard, the second falls unheard.
At night she is sleepless, and if perchance she is overcome
by sleep, she dreams, and her chattering tongue repeats,
"Pear, Pear." If half of her bed is unoccupied,
and Decius isn't there, then is she happy,
and thus she speaks as she lies there alone: 50
"Alas, I do not die, nor yet do I live;

Lidia

I live but, dear Pearus, you're death to me."
Thus she frequently speaks aloud and she sighs;
she groans, and nourishes the wound in her veins.[10]

At long last inspiration finds a cure for her malady;   55
art finds an entrance though which love can pass.
She orders one of her most loyal servants to bear
a message to Pearus, one which Decius must not hear.
The messenger goes on her way and puts Pearus to the test,
speaking flattering words (her mind is full of guile):   60
    "Long life and good health, Pearus; thus does Lidia
often greet you — Lidia whom you could enjoy, in good health,
if you chose to do so. Indeed, she dies for you;
she grows pale and then blushes, and her heart's grief
seeks a lover's solace. For you she sighs,
for you she groans, and you are the reason she languishes   65
in ill heath, and suffers such ills as no one could wish.
She wanders aimlessly by day, in sleep lies dazed,
and is false to her husband. Love of you
kills her, wounds her, burns her."

    Her very first words stupefy Pearus; amazement   70
stops his tongue and his heart trembles with fear.
His mind is driven hither and thither in confusion.
    "Dame Messenger," he says, "you may be just toying with me,
but abandon this wicked game. Away with such sport!
It's not Decius' wife, but Decius himself   75
who's testing my resolve; I love him well,
nor let him think my love is shameful at all.
Lusca,[11] I entreat you, away which such sport
as Lidia wants, for the player gets the blame
when a game like that one turns out badly.
Just as Pearus is faithful, so is Lidia too."

    (Oh easy fidelity — really no fidelity at all!   80
The duke loves her, but she doesn't love him;
he's badly misled, for Lidia leads him
wherever *she* wants, not where *he* wants.
She offers him honeyed words and poisoned deeds.
She's a viper warmed in his loving bosom.

128

Duke, be on your guard! Take care she doesn't bite,   85
for this viper's venom is most deadly of all.
And even if the duke should be on his guard,
she knows well how to beguile him as he watches.
Pretending to play, the tail often does harm.
A woman's guile so beguiles a man that he doesn't   90
look out for himself and neglects his advantage.)

    "Dame messenger, say to your mistress, if she's still
a reasonable woman, that she should be concerned
not with me but with her reputation."
He spoke and groaned aloud, and grief made his voice
catch in mid-speech.

               Lusca returns home,
talking aloud to herself: "Father Hercules,   95
this love madness is different for men and for women.
A woman grows mad; emboldened by lust alone,
she dares to approach, to tempt him, and to do the deed.
She rages and whines like a bitch in heat;
she catches her prey while her modesty escapes.   100
Oh easy morals! One man cannot satisfy such a woman.
Decius isn't enough, nor would ten men be.[12]
All women are the same; what fear did Messalina[13] have?
No woman is afraid; no woman is unwilling;
no, they do the soliciting. Not a one
knows moderation, nor is modesty found in any.   105
When she's on the make, immoderation is all.
Shameful, beautiful, wild, gentle, rich, poor,
she furrows, plows, plucks, shatters, hooks, gapes.[14]
The little girl, preparing for the fight, cuts short her youth;
forgetful of her years, the old crone boils hotly.   110
Each one knows the itch, and is in heat for all —
ah, it is modest to know modesty's work!
I'm amazed and it's really amazing: a woman doesn't care
for what she has. If she has a lot, it's a little she likes.
This one prefers the skinny to the fat, and (oh the shame)   115
that one, having enjoyed a tall man, wants a short one.
Thus Lidia has learned by experience to gratify Decius
in order to prove by a man's art that anyone is a man.

That woman sells herself cheaply; she has no shame.
She's one and the same to all, and nothing to anyone.   120

     The duke's hall is large; because she is shameless
she receives everyone; the doorman issues invitations,
and entrance is easy for the door is wide open.
One after the other arrives and is admitted.
The hammer strikes the anvil three and four times;
she endures the strokes and opens the furnace even wider.   125
She invites Pearus to press upon her thighs;
she asks and he denies; she wants what he rejects
and pays court to the man, a wife false to her husband.
What is marriage now? What has become of the nuptial vow?
What is the advantage of the shared marriage bed?   130
Penelope is nowhere; nowhere is Lucretia of old to be found.
No contemporary woman knows how to be either.
Evil follows hard upon evil, and an illicit law
seems to require Thais to follow hard upon Thais. [15]
There's little enough loyalty today, still less among women.   135
Conduct a survey of them all — you'll find nary a Sabine.
A woman's fidelity to her husband lies only in her face;
if you should look deeper you will find
a gentle zephyr filled with poison.

[LUSCA] "Lusca knows all that Lidia knows;
a woman is familiar with all a woman's tricks.   140
Her lustful infidelity is advantageous for me;
she wouldn't love me nearly so well were she chaste.
How would I ever make money from a stern, sober mistress?
She, however, is flighty, and I therefore have influence.
A sober woman is stingy; even barefaced she fears nothing,   145
but a lustful one is generous with her husband's wealth.
Who cares if Lidia plays around? [16] And afterwards?
What's that to you? Lusca, keep quiet.
This sin which she wants is a good one.
Her husband is indulgent; what do you care
if Lidia plays around? What is it to you
if Decius is left still desirous?   150
She is afraid and hesitates since *I* know her crime.
Even though I loyally keep silent, she thinks

that I speak. She calls me, she talks to me,
and sports in her speech: I am dearer to her
than all the others on account of her game.
The servants all do my will, and I can give orders.   155
Everything is Lusca's, and I am rightly called "One-Eye":
my name is like me and serves as an omen,
just as the moon eclipses the rays of the stars. [17]
Lidia told me once what she knew of my signs;
I forget what she said, something about a constellation.   160
Lusca, do you know why you're called "One-Eye"?
Because, I think, you take your name and omen from the moon.
It was in the fifth month, I admit it, when you emptied
the horns of your mother's womb by being born.
Your star [18] makes you a wanderer,   165
and hence you pass entire nights without sleeping;
you're always in motion. What you do is best done
by night. Light, Lusca, is your enemy,
and the shadow of her name is consistent with slavery.
In your case, the work of art limps somewhat —
you're an unbalanced balance, or a trochee or
some measure with a short and a long foot. [19]   170
You would be plump and round of face, but shame
is to be found in your eyes — though you've got only one.
You know, there's now no beautiful whore in the brothel,
and nevertheless, you know, Lusca is good at this game."

She goes on her way, enjoying her own words,   175
and finds her mistress once more, making free use
in her speech of little pleasantries:
"Lidia, we have lost; the sea's sand is sterile.
We have lost our seed, spilled it upon sterile soil.
He refuses your desire; he doesn't want what you do.
He thinks it unlawful to do that which   180
you ought not to do. His love for his lord
prevents him from testing the love of his lady.
Faithful love serves as a pretext to avoid an intrigue.
You dare, but he is afraid; you are in a hurry
while he is dragging his feet. What you think
is right for you, he thinks wrong to want."

     Saddened by this rejection, Lidia long remained   185
speechless, and wounded to the quick, she groaned deeply.
First blushing, then pallor, changed her face's hue,
as one color erased all trace of the other:
the guilty blush which returned to her face
signals the approach of love, while the pallor
is the sign of her resisting modesty.   190
The inescapable flame burns hot in her innermost marrow;
it shakes her bones, strikes her nerves, hardens her face.
Should she want to speak, her tongue refuses;
a resisting modesty prevents an angry speech.
She doesn't know what to do; her heart is Pearus' only,   195
and out of her mind with love, the lover abandons
herself to love.[20] Lovesick anger, nevertheless,
overcomes her silence, and finally she complains:
"Let us yield, Lusca, at least as long as
the nettle still itches. Look, the injured skin
is still swollen and a delicate pink.   200
Let us yield; after all, violets fade and lilies wither.
the rose which is trampled underfoot in not prized.
Let us yield; perhaps he is ensnared in Mopsus' nets;[21]
nor is he ashamed to have commerce with harlots,
no, he enjoys it! Not otherwise in the spring   205
does one, foraging afield in the gilded countryside
and ignorant of flowers, pluck the foul privet.
The reason why is obvious: Pearus, you tremble in fear
of Decius; it isn't love but fear which prevents you."

     As she speaks the name of Pearus she blushes, then pales;
thus love lays its snares wherever the lover goes.   210
She faints, and sweet grief prevents her from speaking,
and only in the faintest of voices can she express
her heart's desire. No suffering, however, can rid her
of the deadly poison, but it remains in the wound,
wherever the lover goes. When she regains consciousness,   215
she glances sideways at Lusca, and wholly abandoned
to love, implores her aid and advice:
"I want you to know, dear Lusca, as I explain the details,
that no one but you can help me at all.
In your hands lie my life, my hopes, my safety;   220

therefore, I beg, go and speak to the knight.
What impression does a single drop of water make?
The precise moment is important; one is more propitious
than another; the outcome of one hour is better
than that of another. And put persuasion
in your words and a winning smile on your face.   225
Stand so — speak so — place your words so.²²
Promise anything, for promising often gains much;
every love sports more willingly if there's hope of gain."

      Lusca departs, and Lidia imagines in her mind every murmur,
and instructs her deeds in silent deceit.   230
Lusca, shrewd in word and deed, approaches the youth
with a smile, and says the following to him:
"Lidia sighs, and her sighs are all for you,
Pearus. Blind love has opened her eyes;
her body wastes away, and she lies exhausted   235
in body and mind. Passion has weakened
her body, and grief has weakened her heart.
Her ivory complexion grows pale, the beauty of her cheeks
fades, and the flower of flowers no longer blooms
on her cheeks, nor does the rose gleam there any more.
Pearus, the man who fears great things seems no knight;
he whom love inspires is proof against weapons.   240
Pearus, if you wish you can be blessed with wealth and gifts,
and ennoble your knighthood with proud deeds.
Nevertheless, this love has an equal, and goes
equally astray. Pearus is like Hippolytus,
while Lidia is Phaedra. Pearus, you too can come to know
the old ruses and a stepmother's torments,   245
as well as those things which it is better to avoid.
But the virtuous Diana does not avenge every
illicit deed, and only once did a man not escape safely.
A woman can do much, and she knows how to perpetrate
many evils. You know what you have to fear."   250

      Pearus thinks over the fate and death of Hippolytus;
much distressed in his heart he says sadly:
"Either the duke is inattentive or Lidia is out of her mind.
The weak man has a strong wife. But Lusca,

tell me, if Lidia is determined to have her way,   255
how can she succeed in deceiving her husband?"

[LUSCA] "What a question! She rules her husband,
and knows how to prevail; the duke is a fool."

    "Well, Lusca, I shall put your words to the test,"
Pearus said. "If the duke isn't a real man,   260
she should seek a better one in Pearus.
I shall try three tests." And he explains the three:
"The duke has a falcon which he loves very dearly,
and the concern of the illustrjous duke is lavished on
a bird. I want her to kill it.²³ If she refuses,
I won't believe she can easily deceive her husband.   265
And if she also plucks five hairs from his beard,
she will the more swiftly entice the man she tries
to entice by prayers. Finally let her succeed
in extracting one of his teeth. If she does,
she will justly have earned my favors."   270

    Lusca returns: she hastens, she runs, she complains
of delay; but trying to fly, she has to slow down,
and she pants, and she tarries. "Now my Lidia
will have him; now she has him; she is already
at play. Lusca can put down her burden,   275
happy in the outcome of her labor." When she sees
her mistress, she greets her flatteringly:
"Cheers, Lidia, since I return bringing tidings
of good cheer which you will cheerfully cheer.²⁴
Your ship is in port; its sails are dry,
and this time the wind was favorable."   280
She relays the knight's requests. Lidia listens silently,
ravished just as she wants to be ravished.
As soon as her strength has returned, she opens her eyes,
and a rosy hue spreads blushing over her face.
She grows beautiful again; she laughs, and a playful light   285
gleams in her eyes. And joyfully replying
to Pearus' requests, she is all ready for action.

[LIDIA] "Pearus shall have what he asks for, those proofs

he wishes. Has he nothing harder to request?
Let him approach; let him hurry; let him watch.
I want him to experience what a woman can do   290
when she is tormented by the frenzy of love."

    The mind in ignorance does not recognize the signs
of impending disaster, nor in its joy
does it perceive the sorrow to follow.
While Decius sports, while he cheerfully deals
with serious matters, while the halls of the duke
resound with various noises, while the cithers   295
accompany the songs of the people, and while
the harmonious strings of the lyre sing sweetly,
out of the bed chamber, sumptuously attired
comes Lidia.^{25} Jealous, she seizes the bird
as it sits on its perch. "I am worse than this bird,"
she says, "and I am tormented, oppressed, night and day.
It's a disgrace to suffer so many wrongs.   300
The duke prefers the woods to my bedroom,
the grass gives more pleasure than does my bed,
and he likes the wooded glades more than my love.
Well, he'll not do so with impunity, and he shall discover
whether Lidia or a bird has the greater power."
She finished her speech, and she wrings^{26} the bird's neck. 305
He falls breathless. Pearus is dumbfounded,
observing her daring. The rest of the crowd is silent.
He glances at her; their eyes meet.
Laughing she conceals her guile, speaking like this:
"Oh duke, I want you to come into my chamber.   310
Abandon the woods!" As she speaks she entwines
her tender arms around Decius and nuzzles his cheek
with her customary playfulness.
While Lidia sports and nuzzles, while she pretends
to kiss him, she feels the duke's rough beard.
Remembering Lusca's words, she falls on his face;   315
she remembers, and pulls out five hairs.
The duke, as if startled from sleep, rubs the place
now bereft of its hairs, and strokes and touches it.
Then Lidia begins to speak with clever deception
and disarms the duke's reaction with practiced guile.   320

"These untimely white hairs lie about your age
and make you seem old before your time.
That beard which was an unseemly black and white,
even though you are young — why look, now it's
a harmonious monochrome." So she spoke,
and she calms him down by throwing her arms   325
about his neck, embracing him in a way he enjoys.
The duke is disarmed by caresses and false love
and doesn't rebuke his wife for her deeds.
Pearus laughs, and Lidia changes her temper;
now love replaces her former fear.   330
And, although she keeps silent, her mind
speaks within; she fears, replies, complains.[27]
The woman caresses the man with a viper's venom;
she's a Chimera to be gaped at with her wiles.
Now she's a lion, now a serpent, now a she-goat —   335
ferocious, untrustworthy, horrible.
A triple monster, a threefold deceit.
Filled with artifice, relying upon deceit, confident in vice,
she manipulates feelings, excites hearts, joins mouths.
What strange law designed her? Nature went astray.
Lo the rabbit turns hound, the wolf becomes a billy-goat.   340
The mouse pretends to be a cow, and the bald monkey
thinks it's a camel.[28] The mole laughs
to see the eyes of the lynx. Air, earth, sea —
all throw up monstrous creatures but only one,
woman (how I shudder!), gives birth to multiple monstrosities.

Lidia, although beset by cares, tastes her joys   345
in advance, although she delays their accomplishment.
Watchful by day and by night, she plots more and more
to find a way to extract one of Decius' teeth.
Finally she finds her chance and accosts the noble youths
whose custom it is to bear the duke's cup.   350
"We know that you," she says, "are scions of a noble race,
but you do not know how low you have sunk.
I think you have perceived the evil and are really ashamed,
but it remains hidden; the vase doesn't reveal its flaw.
When you offer me the cup, your bad breath
infects the cup not a little with its stench.   355

136

Therefore, I advise you, when you offer the wine
to the duke, to step backwards and turn your faces away
so your breath does not disturb the liquor of Bacchus,
and he, having discovered the problem, become enraged." 360

    The young men think over the advice they have heard;
whether it is true or not, naively they are afraid.
They depart, and shame keeps their mouths tight closed,
and they grow pale in turns. The pretense
ensures the success of the trick.
Each tests the mouth of the other for odors, 365
and, finding nothing, says he's found something:
"Stand still! The smell comes from an infected palate.
Your teeth are fine, but your tongue
is vilely inflamed." Another touches the throat,
and finally pronounces: "You have a black tooth here;
that's the source of the ill." 370
The third sniffs in another's mouth, but perceives
no trouble there, yet he makes himself
partner to the conspiracy.
Thus error puts error to the test,
and each begins to fear for himself.

    Meanwhile the youths are ordered to wait upon Decius; 375
it chanced to be a joyous festival of Jove.
There was a great commotion. The hall was adorned
with luxurious accouterments; the cuisine is
worthy of praise. The young men are ready
to serve the wine, but each, when he holds the goblet, 380
turns his head to the side. Everyone is amazed.
The duke is silent before this spectacle
which repeats itself many times, and pretends
that he hasn't seen what he really has.
Finally, for he doesn't want secrets to remain 385
hidden, he asks his wife to explain this mystery.
She summons a sickly pallor up into her face
(though inwardly rejoicing), and sadly she says:
"Up to now this was a secret of the bed chamber,
known to Lidia alone, but now everyone speaks of it — 390
the very walls echo this ill abroad.

I am in a quandary; I don't know what to do —
whether to speak or to keep silence."

The duke replies, "Lidia, tell me all."

[LIDIA] "But with what countenance, with what voice
am I to express your shame (nay, really my own)?
Do you truly want me to explain?"

"I do," said the duke. And with a tearful face   395
she begins to speak, having found her chance
to deceive. "Your mouth, my lord, emits a stench.
The youths have perceived this. I speak,
although they keep silent."

                     Decius is amazed.
He sighs. He weakly tries to speak,
but breaks off; his voice loses its way.   400
He strokes his throat, opens his mouth and exhales.
Scarcely can the duke believe it himself.
"What will you advise me to do; Lidia, what's your plan?
What art or what medecine will come to my aid?"

      "If your tooth offend you," said Lidia,   405
"pluck it out! If this is the cause
of your ill, get it out of your mouth."

     "Let some one stronger than I come here," said
Lusca (for she was their companion). "My strength
isn't enough to pull it out."

                "Whose aid
do you seek?" asked the duke.

                    Lidia said, "Pearus's.
He's faithful to you, and will be strong enough."   410

    Pearus is summoned. Lusca reveals
what Lidia has in mind, the trick by which
the duke is to be duped. They enter the bed chamber

where Lidia, wrestling with the tooth,
strikes and pushes and pulls her poor husband.
"Pearus, what's this? What are you doing?   415
Look how wearily Lidia toils," urges Lusca.
"Let's help her, quick!"

                   Oh, how much pain
assails the man, how much toil the woman!
The duke groans and grieves, perhaps at
the sight of his bloody face. Shaken by the assault
he jumps up. At long last the tooth
is pulled out and leaps right out of his mouth.   420
She who has ravished him in deeds repays him in words
so he won't grieve any more, yet still he grieves.

    Pearus departs, scarcely able to repress his laughter.
He reacts to the fulfillment of his wishes
with the following words: "Greatest father of the gods,   425
you who have obliterated the former age,
giving the world a second chance through Deucalion,
you may think you are all-knowing, but you don't know
Lidia alone, nor are her doings apparent.
Neither Niobe in pride, nor Circe in magic,
nor Medea in wickedness, nor Lais in fickleness,   430
nor she who with a blind murmur turned her gaze
from Phlegethon's streams,[29] not a one is Lidia's equal!"

    Scarcely had he finished this soliloquy
when Lusca burst out of the chamber, convulsed
with laughter, and she said, raising high her hands:
"What do you think of the duke? What do you think   435
now, Pearus? Lidia can do anything,
of that you can be sure. Decius lacks a tooth,
and what's more, he's lost everything.
You are not the one Lidia mocks, I Lusca
assure you of that. She's already on her way,
and then the deed will prove whether you,
Pearus, are really male or female."

    She had finished her speech. The other woman   440

approaches, more beautiful than Tyndareus' daughter,[30]
fairer than she for whom Jupiter
made double that celebrated night.[31]
In her face the hue of lily and rose;
her eyes reveal the gleam of twin stars.
Her lips are playful, a lascivious libation to love.   445
She sports and invites joys as sweet as honey.
Her hair is artistically decorated with gold,
but that gold is rivaled by the gold of her hair.
On her bosom gleams a necklace of flashing gems
which outshines the very rays of the sun.   450
She wears a rosy cloak with a golden fringe
embroidered with brilliant gems.
She approaches and steals Pearus' heart with her eyes;
ravished, she ravishes him with her ravishing beauty.
She approaches, and her loving gaze   455
both caresses and beseeches him to accede.
Whatever there is in her gaze urges making a treaty.
She approaches and seeks Pearus, and extracts
from him a pledge of good health; she presses
his hand with her hand, and coming closer
points out to him that most private chamber
where joys are to be found.   460

When the deed is done, Pearus says to her,
"Lidia, I marvel. You can do marvelous things.
Everything you do is a marvel. While other women
hesitate, Lidia, you fear nothing. What no other woman
can do, you alone bring to pass."   465

[LIDIA] "All this is nothing, Pearus. You have not
seen a thing. Now you will see what Lidia
really can do! For I know that the duke
can be deceived. Should he really see something,
he will think he's seen nothing. Why,
if he should catch me *in flagrante delicto*,
he wouldn't believe his eyes. I want this,   470
and therefore I forbid any objection."

"Lidia, those three former tests were nothing,"

says Pearus, "unless you add this fourth to them."

      She explained how it could be done, and by what art
the crime could be perpetrated. She instructs him
in the time and the place. Then they separate,
and return home. When the kissing is finished,   475
Pearus regains his dwelling; Lidia, delighted,
rejoins her husband. The question arises,
will another tooth grow to replace the one
the duke has lost? This Lidia can deny,
but Lusca confesses that an old man   480
can have a new tooth, whereupon Lidia concludes:
"If an old man can hope, why not a young one?"
The duke is comforted by this reply; he waits,
but in vain, the fulfillment of his wishes.

      Having completed her plans, Lidia pretends to be sick.   485
She willingly counterfits disease's discomforts;
her veins throb; the doctor takes her pulse
but misses the mark. Her disease is ambiguous,
and passion, when it wants, can be deceiving.
She burns at will with a fever, then suffers chills   490
and is faint. Thus playful love deludes,
and Lidia deceives the doctor with her evil art,
and her husband she dupes by guile and deceit.

      There was a garden surrounded by water,
thick with shade trees, fertile with sweet fruits.
A fountain flowed in the middle, shaded by   495
the branches of a pear tree which proferred
real joy in the spring. To relieve the heat of her fever
(the ardor of vice), Lidia comes here,
joyful in deceit. Both the duke and Pearus
accompany the "sick" woman on her journey.
She gives Pearus her right hand, the duke her left.   500
Lusca brings up the rear, laughing and talking
to herself, delighted with the way the ruse is working.
Her lips curve up into a smile, and at Decius[32]
she makes the gesture of the crane,[33]
while the sick woman stumbles along.

They come to a halt. The spot accords well with love.   505
All praise the flowers, the plashing fountain.
Their eyes reveal desire, and they sigh.
The duke says, "Pearus, climb up and pick some pears."
Pearus mounts to the top of the tree.
Lusca remarks, "Now, Pearus, strike the pear   510
with a better one."[34] Lidia, looking up,
gazes upon Pearus in the pear tree:
love's fruit is in the fruit of that tree.

"Oh, I beg you," calls out Pearus, "my duke, spare me,
spare my modesty. This is not the place
to make love! This love is impetuous.
This is not a healthy passion!   515
Lidia, my lord, go elsewhere to pant out your passion.
My lord, you have chambers appropriate to this sport.
Go to it, but let me not observe this uncourtly[35] deed."

Decius wonders what this ridiculousness means,
while Lusca laughs and bites her fingers to stop.   520
"The tree is at fault," says Lidia, sighing;
"heights often distort what one sees."

The duke says, "Come down quickly, come down.
Why do you delay?"

Pearus responds,
"All right, but spare my modesty."
Pearus climbs down and says, "Duke, please!"   525
He entreats, as if the other was unwilling;
"spare me," he repeats.

The duke says,
"I shall put this to the test, for often
fantasy deceives us; is it Pearus or the pear
tree who is making fun of me?"
The duke and Pearus mount simultaneously,
both breathing hard; the one insinuates himself   530
among the branches, the other between thighs.
Both labor hard, but one enjoys his work.

While the one shakes the pear tree, the other
strikes the thigh. Decius is amazed,
and uncomprehending but gullible, hardly believes his eyes.
The more he gapes uncertain, the clearer it is
what is going on. He takes it in and doubts;   535
he trembles and groans. He lies in wait;
scarcely believing his eyes, he waits.
"Either it's the real thing," he says, "or I am deceived.
He seems to be fanning the fire, or else though awake
I think I am dreaming. I don't know
if he has deceived me; I think it was all a trick."   540
Decius ascribes it to the branches, and breaks them
and shakes them. Frequently Pearus is assalted
with pears thrown down from the pear tree.
Then both Pearus and the duke swiftly climb down,
each one eager to deceive the other.   545

     "Either I am crazy," says the duke,
"or I am deceived by this undertaking."

Lidia: "Pearus didn't move me; it was the pears."

[PEARUS] "I confess I saw what he thinks to see.
I saw and I thought it was true,
but now I see more clearly; it was nothing at all."   550

[LIDIA] "As I told you, duke, it was the tree's fault,
and perhaps it will make fun of others hereafter.
The danger remains. Since the shadow
causes such evil, let the tree be cut down."

     The duke gives the order. The tree is chopped down.
Lusca conceals her smiles, and Pearus   555
covers his pears, and Lidia her belly.
One man is made unhappy by the deceit of three.

Notes to *Lidia*

1. Translated from the text of Edmond Lackenbacher, in Cohen, I, pp. 226-46.

2. A reference to another twelfth-century "comedy," the *Miles Gloriosus* (The Braggart Knight).

3. *Lidiades*, a coinage on the model of Ovid's *Heroides*; the word is glossed in the MSS, *comedia de Lidia facta*, "the comedy made about Lidia."

4. By giving his scabrous piece a seemingly didactic purpose, Arnulf apparently seeks to avoid censure; a similar motive is frequently ascribed to Ovid in medieval *accessus* to his works, which claim that he depicted evil women only so men would know what to avoid.

5. The Latin is *Pyrrhus*, a name which involves a pun on the homonym, *pirus*, "pear tree," as well as the proper name. I have chosen "Pearus" as the closest approximation in English.

6. A reference to Vitalis of Blois' comedy, *Geta*.

7. For a discussion of this invective, see the studies of Roy and Bertini, 1978. The "jealous one" is probably to be identified with Matthew of Vendôme.

8. In medieval belief Apollo, but in classical mythology really the sun; Ovid tells the story in *Metamorphoses* 2.

9. The pun in Latin on *virus* "virus" and *virum* "man," "husband" is neater.

10. A quotation from Vergil, *Aeneid* 4.1-2, describing the lovesick Dido.

11. The name means "one-eyed"; I cannot find a suitable English equivalent to serve as a name for the go-between.

12. A pun on *Decius* and *decem* "ten."

13. The wife of the Roman emperor Claudius, noted for her debauchery.

14. The violence attributed to the woman in love is typical of both classical and medieval thought.

15. A common name for a prostitute; see *Babio,* n. 12.

16. One of Arnulf's favorite wordplays is on the name of his heroine and *ludus, ludere* "play," "to play." The pun is cannot be reproduced in English.

17. The moon, or rather the man-in-the-moon, is said to have only one eye since he appears in profile; see the note of J. M. Crawford, p. 72.

18. The moon.

19. These lines are somewhat obscure. Compare, however, the description of the limping slave Spurius in *Alda,* 187-88.

20. The play on *amens* "mad" and *amans* "loving" is proverbial.

21. The name of a shepherd in Vergil's *Eclogues.*

22. This line, meaningless in a written text, could be very funny in a mimed performance.

23. All three of Pearus' requests involve symbolic forms of castration. The falcon was a popular symbol in the Middle Ages for male sexual prowess; see Lacy, p. 354.

24. The use in these lines of five words employing the same root, *salus* "health" is excessive in English but the height of poetic good form in the Middle Ages.

25. The length of this period, with six consecutive *dum* clauses ("while"), of which I have retained five, is remarkable. Arnulf is showing off.

26. I have kept the tenses of the original.

27. The text is corrupt here.

145

28. The references are to well-known fables.

29. This allusion has not been identified.

30. Helen.

31. Alcmena.

32. A derisive gesture in which one points a finger bent in the shape of a crane's beak; see Persius, *Satire* 1.52.

33. The meaning of the verb *cimbalat* in unclear, but presumably it refers to making a noise like cymbals.

34. Du Cange (5.266) notes that "pear" can mean "testicle."

35. The Latin is *rusticus*, "churlish"; in works like Andreas Capellanus' *The Art of Courtly Love*, the word for "courtly" is *urbanus*, the opposite (following Ovid) of *rusticus*.

THE THREE GIRLS

I chanced to go down a road alone one day,[1]
and Love, just as usual, was my only companion.
And as I walked, I was composing some verses,
musing on a girl to whom to send the poems,[2]
when, lo, at a distance, I saw what seemed to be   5
three fair nymphs coming towards me,
of whom one, I recall, was the tallest.
This girl happened to be running in the center,
and though they all ran equally well,
yet she ran the best; and if perchance
she had held in her hands a bow and arrow,
she would surely have seemed to be Diana,   10
for thus that goddess is accustomed to hunt
the wild beasts throughout the dark forest,
and thus she runs with her maidens.
Then wishing to know them and learn their names,
I began to hasten, in a hurry to meet them.
And as I came closer, I noted each one,   15
and seeing their faces (hidden before),
I discovered that they were not nymphs at all
but lovely young women, though I hardly think
that the sea goddesses can be nearly as fair.
Scarcely could I compare Venus, or Juno,
or beautiful Pallas with these lovely maidens.   20
Soon their faces, soon their long flowing hair,
soon their bodies, soon their hands, their fingers —
all pleased me, for Cupid had fixed deep
in my heart his arrows and his blazing torches.

Between the three had arisen a quarrel   25
as to which was most skilled at song
(for of course one was the most skillful).
Therefore the three were running along
so that one of them might bear away
from an impartial judge victory's palm.
The first carried roses, the second an apple,[3]
the third a branch, for these are three things   30

which often give delight to young maidens.

    To describe one of the three is well worth my while,
for one of the three was by far the most fair.
Her garments shimmered with gold and with jewels,
but her body's splendor outshone them all.
Her hair was flaxen, girt about with gleaming gold,   35
but her hair pleased me far more than the gold.
She wore a crown of roses in full bloom on her head
(a head which would have been nonetheless
utterly splendid without any adornment).
Her lovely forehead, her milky-white throat,
her neck and her hands have inflamed many hearts,
but mine they have inflamed forever.   40
In the calm night's sky the shining stars
glow no brighter than did the stars of her eyes.
Upon her ears she wore magnificent jewels
set in gold (ears, however, which little deserved
to be burdened with so great a weight).
I could not discern the shape of her breasts,   45
either because they were too small or because
they were bound up — girls frequently bind their breasts
with bands, for too buxom a bosom men
do not find enticing — but this girl, my girl,
does not have to resort to such measures,
for her bosom by nature is quite nicely small.   50
Her girdle was gorgeous, studded with gems and gold,
encircling the graceful body of my fair lady.

    But why should I mention each separate part?[4]
If I should mention each separate part,
I do not think that a thousand days
would suffice — no, I hardly think so at all.
And if some parts remained veiled from my view,   55
they seemed still better than all the rest[5]
(and I know for a fact that the best were concealed).

    But what should I do? I did not dare
to be the first to utter a word,
but Love compelled me to speak, so I said:

"Hail, queen of your companions, woman or goddess,
you are most worthy of my salutation.   60
Greetings as well to your companions, among whom
you, maiden, delight me the most. If perchance
some cause for strife has arisen between you
I'll settle your quarrel by my arbitration.
You may with justice submit to my judgment   65
for I'm an expert on every good art.
                    [*a line is missing*]
I have been well schooled in the art of song."

        As soon as they heard my mention of song,
the maidens leapt forward, and each one was
saying at once, "You will be *my* judge."   70

        We saw a lovely meadow, abloom with flowers,
in the midst of which there stood an oak tree
in whose shade we found it pleasant
to hold our trial of song. Here on the soft turf
I was the first to sit down, and I instructed   75
each girl to take her place on the grass.
Then I bade the maiden who carried the roses
to sing the first; thus ordered, she sang the first.
She sang of Jupiter's desperate battles,   80
his fierce fights with the giants,
and told how they perished in Jove's mighty blaze.
When she'd finished her song, immediately the second girl
(the one with the branch) got up from the grass.
Standing in our midst, she sang of Paris' love
(for this was the song she knew the best).
Scarcely had she finished when — at long last —   85
the third maiden (for still the third maiden remained)
began her song, and, her hair crowned with flowers,
standing before us, with her hand she bade us be silent.
She sang of Jupiter, of his tender, amorous smiles,
and how he sported with his fair Europa.   90
Her voice, pleasing to all, pleased me all the more
for I was the only one to give her pleasure.
Each time the sound poured out from her rosy lips,
the surrounding rocks re-echoed the sound.

149

Not otherwise long ago among the Ismarian hills   95
did Orpheus sing, accompanying himself on the lyre.
Thus too the Sirens are said to have sung
when they wished to detain the Ithacan's ships —
each one by her song contriving to prevent
Ulysses' departure — but all the same
they could not detain that guileful hero.   100
But what if my lady's had been the voice
that hero had heard? Why, only she
could have succeeded in staying him with song.

    When she'd finished her song, her voice falling silent,
I immediately began my praise of her singing.
And as in my judgment she'd defeated her rivals,   105
I said: "It's my verdict that you are the winner;
by your voice you surpass your companions,
and not by voice only but also by beauty.
Therefore to you must I give a double crown,
together with highest praise, for you have won,
oh victorious maiden, a two-fold victory."   110
Then making a twin crown from an assortment of flowers,
I placed it on her head, a reward she richly deserved.
Meanwhile she too was charmed by a secret love,
but the other two were most grieved at her honor.
Then she said: "Oh youth who has honored me   115
so greatly, great rewards are owing to you.
And so that you may know what your merit is,
and may put to the test the bonds of my friendship,
ask of me whatever reward you find pleasing.
I shall give it to you; you may have whatever you want.   120
And do not think that I am deceitful; you can be sure
that my promises have weight. I swear
by the sacred sceptre of Jove that the promises
which I have made I will keep."

             [a line is missing]

    " You promise great rewards for my merits, maiden,"   125
I said, "and I shall indeed expect a great
reward. Now I ask you, I beg you,

my only wish is to be united with you,
if you are willing, for you please me greatly.
No gift, I swear it, could be more precious than you.
Give me yourself; you'll have given me everything.   130
When Venus, Pallas, and Juno sought Paris out,
each goddess offered him her own reward.
When they'd named their gifts for him,
he chose the best of the three (you know the story),
that he should be given the most beautiful bride.
If he'd known something more precious   135
than a beautiful girl, that would he have chosen.
His example teaches us what gift's to be sought;
following his example, my fair one,
you are what I seek, just as Paris feared not
to prefer Venus to the other two,
for she gave him the young Helen as his prize.   140
Since you defeated the other two with my aid,
so grant me, I beg, your virginity for my enjoyment.
But should I seem unworthy of so great a reward,
there is something else you can give me
and still preserve your maidenhead intact.
If, therefore, you are unwilling to give me   145
this ultimate gift, the affair can remain
superficial, and still offer pleasure to me."[8]

    There was no delay. Smiling tenderly at me,
the modest virgin replied: "Do not worry,"
she said, seeing my hesitation, "I alone
will be joined with you alone in passion.   150
You will be mine; I will give you my maidenhead,
for I have kept this honor — my virginity — just for you.
And lest you have to wait, tormented by doubt,
this very night shall you gain your promised reward."
She spoke, and advising her comrades to make ready,   155
she directed her swift steps toward her castle.

    Already Phoebus had touched the deep ocean with his chariot
when my lady entered her chambers. I was not sure
(though she had sworn) that she really wished
to give herself to me by the law of the bed.   160

151

And wishing to put her to the test (there was
no harm in trying), I devised this stratagem:
pretending that I desired to return home,
I said, "Maiden, wait, I must go; farewell."

Immediately giving me the most delectable kisses,   165
she said: "Here for you dinner is prepared with us.
Here might you also taste the shared bliss of my bed,
and here might one Venus, one passion, unite us.
Night, full of shadows, is coming on;
night now holds the whole world fast,
nor does the moon shine serenely in her sky.   170
There is no gate open through which to depart,
nor can you go home alone through the shadows.
Often, indeed, the spirits of the night endanger
those who persist in traveling by night.
On the one hand night, on the other love,   175
both keep you from going, and I am the third,
as I strive to detain you by means of my prayers.
I entreat you now, don't let my prayers be in vain.
I marvel if we three — night, love, and a beautiful girl —   180
if we three cannot restrain a single man.
Dear one, stay, I beg, and soon you will know
love's passionate fires if your heart be not steel."

I granted my lady's prayers and her wishes,
for that which pleased her was not exactly
displeasing to me, since now I knew well   185
that she did not despise me, for if she had
she would not have begged me to stay.

Dinner was ready; the meat smoked on all sides;
on all sides tables were placed⁹ at the couches.
[*a line missing*]
Men servants and maid servants completed their tasks;   190
this one brought water, another bore platters;
yet another set out the goblets,
each one striving at his task to give satisfaction.
We sat down to eat (the meal was exceptionally good),
but the dinner gave me no satisfaction

for every time I gazed at my lady's eyes and her face,   195
my body began to burn with a delightful fire.
Oh, how many times did I groan,
oh, how many times did I sigh,
seeing the smiles that she gave me!
Her smiles were bliss, but to tell the truth
they caused me much grief; then did I suffer   200
great pain; then was I unable to sate my body
with the delicacies set out in abundance for me.

[*a line missing in which she offers him a roasted dove*]

She spoke, first giving me several kisses:
"My dear, eat these thighs which I offer you *now*,   205
and later tonight I'll offer you mine;
I'm offering you a great gift, for in bearing my thighs
you'll bear a great prize, if you really do want it."

Taking the thighs, I ate the bones with the flesh,
and never was there food any sweeter to me.   210
Had she offered me even inferior meats,
they'd have seemed just as delicious.
She praised my deed and gave me a golden cup;
I took it up and drank from the spot ^{10}
which her rosy lips had touched before.
Only in this fashion could I be satisfied   215
by the food and drink which before left me wanting.

Dinner was over. After dinner the tables were removed.
My lady ordered everyone to prepare his own bed,
but the servants, bawling drunken hymns to Bacchus,
made beds neither for themselves nor for us.   220
They staggered off, overcome by wine and by sleep,
nor did husband and wife remember the other.
One lies down on top of the hay, another beneath it;
yet another stetches out on a blanket of straw.
I sought the bed of my lady, and my lady went with me;   225
she sought her domain, and I was her chosen companion.
The bed gladly welcomed our two young bodies —
a bed which was not large yet embraced us both.

An artist's hand had carved that bed with wondrous skill,
and on it he'd painted the gods with their ladies.   230
Jupiter was there laughing, deceiving virgins;
some he deceived disguised as a swan, others as an eagle.
Indeed the artist had painted the god in so many shapes
that one found it hard to believe in his divinity.
Elsewhere he'd painted with utmost skill   235
Venus and Mars embracing naked in bed.
There too I saw Vulcan extending his net
in order to catch them embracing in bed.
Indeed I feared that he wanted to catch us too,
so realistically had the painter portrayed him.   240
And when I had laughed at my fear, my lady
laughed too, but laughter became her far better than me.

  Why do I delay? I lay down on the bed
and covered my limbs with an embroidered quilt.
Then my lady ordered her maids out of the room   245
and fastened the bolt on the bedroom door.
On all sides the fire gleamed from golden lamps
as though the sun pranced inside with his horses of gold.
She undressed; indeed, she wanted me to see her naked,[11]
for there was not a blemish on her delicate body.   250
Now believe me you lovers, if you want to believe!
Her body was whiter than snow,
not snow which, touched by Phoebus, has melted,
but that snow which as yet no sun has warmed.
Ah, what shoulders did I see,   255
and gleaming thighs that were just as fair.
Her lovely breasts were small, perfect for love
(if a little bit firm, nonetheless just right for me).
Small was her waist, taut the belly beneath,
and rounded hips gave alluring curves to her figure.   260
I shall not tell you what next I saw,
although I could describe far better sights if I wished —
no, not a word — but I could hardly restrain myself,
seeing her naked, from seizing her milky-
white body with a hot lustful hand.
What should I do? I could no longer look   265
nor yet could I gaze too long on that radiant body.

The more I gazed, the more enflamed with passion I grew,
the sight tormenting but delighting me too.
But when I had looked long enough at her lovely body
(I gazed long, for she well deserved my long gaze),   270
she climbed into bed, quite ready for love,
and lifting the quilt with her hand, covered our bodies.
Straightway pressing my lips to her glowing neck,
I began to devour my lady with passionate kisses.
I gave her then a thousand kisses   275
and she returned the same number to me —
a thousand given, a thousand returned.
She pressed her side to my side;
my side rejoiced at the touch of her body.
Then she pressed my belly with hers
and sought a thousand such ways to delight me.   280

"Love, she said, do your will with me,[12] do it swiftly,
for black night is fleeing, day returning."
Then she asked for my hand, and I stretched it out.
She placed it on her breasts and she said:
"What, my dearest love, do you feel now?"

While I held her, I replied in this way: 285
"I feel," I said, "a prize which greatly delights me.
Now I hold that reward which I have always desired,
and how greatly have I desired
that reward which now I hold."
Then moving my hand from her breasts,
I stroked her youthful thighs;
she was then sweeter than honey to me.   290
I said at once, "There is no gold more precious,
there is nothing in the world more delectable than you.
I greatly enjoyed the thighs of the dove that you fed me,
but now I touch thighs I enjoy even more.
Therefore let us join our bodies together;   295
united as one, let us embrace closely,
and let our bodies play their parts well."

What to do now? I would tell you what then
transpired, but modesty prevents me,

155

The Three Girls

and my lady forbids me to speak.
The conclusion remains. Did it turn out well?
Love knows all, and Venus does too. 300

Notes to *The Three Girls*

1. Translated from the edition by Pittaluga (Bertini, 1976); see also the edition of Maury in Cohen, II, pp. 232-42. The opening of the poem echoes Horace, *Satires* 1.9, "Ibam forte via sacra..." (I chanced to be going along the Sacred Way).

2. Like Ovid at the opening of the *Amores*, the poet is a love-poet who has not yet found a suitable addressee for his verses.

3. This girl, the heroine of the poem, is carrying a love token common in antiquity (*cf.*, for example, the apple of the judgment of Paris).

4. A quotation from Ovid, *Amores* 1.5.23, "Why should I mention each separate part? I saw nothing not worthy of praise."

5. So Apollo thought of Daphne; Ovid, *Metamorphoses* 1.502, "Siqua latent, meliora putat" (If anything is concealed, he thinks it better).

6. The reader properly familiar with his Ovid (that is, the intended audience of this poem), would realize from the first singer's choice of subject that she will not win the contest. In *Amores* 2.1, Ovid depicts himself as having been engaged in writing a gigantomachy when his girlfriend became angered with him, and he therefore abandoned this grandiose epic subject and returned to amatory poetry.

7. The verb *luserat* can mean both "play" and "deceive." The third maiden is a proper Ovidian, for Ovid tells this story in *Metamorphoses* 2.833ff.

8. That is, should the girl be unwilling "to go all the way," a form of love known in medieval erotic casuistry as *amor mixtus* (defined by Andreas Capellanus [trans. Parry, p. 122] as "that which gets its effect from every delight of the flesh and culminates in the final act of Venus"), the lover is prepared to accept *amor purus*, described by Andreas as going "as far as the kiss and the embrace and the modest contact with the nude lover, omitting the final solace. . . ." In Andreas, the woman's response to her suitor's offer of *amor purus* is: "You are saying things that no one ever heard or knew of, things

that one can scarcely believe. I wonder if anyone was ever found with such continence that he could resist the promptings of passion and control the actions of his body" (p. 123).

9. The Latin switches here to the present tense, and thereafter tenses are mixed for the sake of the meter. I maintain the past tense.

10. As Ovid does, *Amores* 1.4.33.

11. From here on the poem is a conscious adaptation and amplification of Ovid, *Amores* 1.5, except that the medieval maiden does not share Corinna's coy (and feigned) modesty.

12. This maiden does not adhere to the Ovidian tenet that that women prefer physical compulsion to voluntary submission (*Ars Amatoria* 1.673-74); the girl's words, however, more closely echo Venus' adaptation of Ovid in *Pamphilus* than they do the actual Ovidian passage.